The Art of Mental Resilience

A Practical Guide to Overcoming Life's Adversities and Challenges.

Ives Y. Murai

To Yumi.

Without your support, I wouldn't be here right now.

Contents

SIGN UP FOR MY NEWSLETTER

JOIN MY NEWSLETTER

If you'd like up-to-date information on new releases and promotions, consider signing up for my newsletter. Visit my website at https://ivesymurai.com.

INTRODUCTION

You've been told a lie. Everything you think you know about resilience is wrong. "Bold claim," you might be thinking. Maybe your definition of resilience is associated with having thick skin. The thing is, I also had many misconceptions about mental resilience. My first misconception was that having thick skin equaled being resilient and not caring about what others thought or said about me. The second misapprehension was that being thick-skinned or mentally tough was the same as having an immunity to fear, embarrassment, sadness, or anger. Thirdly and finally, I believed you're either born thick-skinned or you're not. Boy, how wrong I was.

Let me tell you a secret: being resilient actually means being capable of adapting to adversities. It means behaving and reacting to adversity in a way that furthers your goals, not counters them. Being resilient means that it's totally okay and normal to feel sad, sorry, concerned, or annoyed. These feelings are healthy—they help you get things done. By extension, feeling anger, self-pity, panic, and depression are unhealthy feelings; they will probably affect you and your goals negatively. Finally, even if you are not born resilient, you can improve your resilience.

So yes, having thick skin doesn't equate to mental or emotional resilience. Yet, many people think that having thick skin is great. After all, why wouldn't it be? Someone you know could say something unpleasant to you to try to deliberately hurt you. In response, you would just shrug it off and continue about your day. You would probably forget by lunchtime that they said something nasty right before you left for work. Or so people who have thick skin claim. Hint: that's not completely true.

The above sounds really good, though, doesn't it? Especially if you suffer from anxiety, depression, or unhelpful thought patterns like rumination, or, more precisely, "Obsessional thinking involving excessive, repetitive thoughts or themes that interfere with other forms of mental activity...)"[1]

Maybe you believe you possess thin skin and get upset at the comments you hear from those in your social circle. You believe that things your family members, friends, and the occasional coworker say shouldn't make you so upset. So why do you feel so troubled by it? Why do social cues sometimes seem like they're designed to disturb your peace of mind?

How often do you think to yourself, "Why am I so stressed out?" "Why is my life so full of difficulties?" or "Why do such little things make me so upset?" These thoughts indicate there's an opportunity to improve your mental resilience. After all, your performance at school, university, or work may depend on how resilient you are. Not only that, but your resilience will also affect your health and relationships. Many psychologists go so far as to say that your resilience directly influences your happiness and success, so why neglect it?

After reading this book, you'll be able to not only meet problems head-on but be in a better position after you deal with them, ready for whatever comes your way next. You will be able to deal with stress, anxiety, unhelpful thinking patterns, and the nasty things people say to you in a much healthier way than what you're used to. You will still feel negative feelings, but they won't have the same tight grip on your emotional health as they used to. You will look back, after all that hard work it took to implement the concepts in this book and think, "I'd do it again!"

What This Book Will Teach You

In this book, you will learn everything you need to know to improve your mental resilience:

- What being resilient really means.
- How your feelings, thoughts, and behaviors are interconnected.
- The real benefits of being mentally resilient.
- The meaning and importance of irrationalities.
- How to analyze the most important aspects of adversities so you can accurately handle them.
- The most effective techniques to use when facing life obstacles.
- How to handle difficult situations in major life areas.
- A step-by-step guide to increase resilience.

What This Book Will Not Teach You

This book was not written to give you a motivation boost, nor will it teach you how to improve your motivation. You will not find any stories with impossible odds describing how a brave soul found a magic way of getting rid of life problems and never felt sad or angry ever again. There are thousands of books better suited for that need.

It will not teach you how to stop feeling depressed, angry, guilty, ashamed, or any other strong emotion. It's impossible. Your brain cannot switch these emotions off.

I won't try to teach you esoteric techniques to make yourself feel better. You won't hear a single word about methods to increase your self-esteem or confidence. Although they do have their uses, I won't talk about self-affirmations in this book either.

What This Book Is and What This Book Is Not

This is a guide to help you deal with adversities in a healthy, rational way. When you handle your problems rationally and behave rationally, you increase your resilience. You may not feel it immediately, as it is a slow process. But by reading this guide, you'll be on the right path to self-improvement.

I believe science has a lot to offer to society, although I don't believe science has the last word on everything. For that reason, I'm confident, not only from my own experience but also from the amount of scientific knowledge available, that science provides one of the best ways to deal with challenges in life. That's why I try to provide sources for the many concepts present in this book. Just keep in mind that this book is not a scientific work.

Take Action Now

So now you know what to expect and what not to expect from this book. It will teach you how to improve your resilience. It will teach you effective techniques to help you deal with stress whenever you're confronted with obstacles. When you've finally read everything, take action to practice the most fundamental aspects presented here. It won't be easy, but you probably already know that things, especially the most important to us, don't come easy in life.

Let's first define resilience. Ready? Then read on.

---

1. American Psychological Association, *APA Dictionary of Psychology*, 2nd ed. (Washington, DC: American Psychological Association, 2015), 626.

Chapter One

What is Resilience?

> It's not what happens to you, but how you react to it that matters.
>
> —Epictetus, Greek philosopher

Welcome to the first chapter of the book. This chapter will go over the meaning of resilience, the biological factors behind irrationality, common sources of disturbance, and rational emotive behavioral therapy.

At the height of the Russia-Ukraine conflict, sometime in the first half of 2022, when all the media outlets were focused on the invasion of Ukraine by the Russian forces, my brain, for some reason, thought that a new world war was imminent, and that was a perfect moment to start having a panic attack. I remember the moment it started, the difficulty in breathing, the inability to focus on anything, the pressure in my chest, the feeling of impending doom. Fortunately, I was working from home and had no classes scheduled. My coworker, another victim of anxiety, tried to calm me down through online chat. Only after using a couple of relaxation techniques was I able to finally slow down and end the panic attack. I then began to wonder if I could have avoided the panic attack by being more emotionally resilient.

So, what in the world is resilience? What does it mean to have mental resilience or be emotionally strong? Simply put, it's the ability to handle your emotions when something disturbs your inner peace. That could be the end of a long-term relationship, losing your job, or learning that someone close to you has cancer or another potentially life-threatening health condition.

Here's the definition of resilience taken from the APA Dictionary of Psychology:

> The process and outcome of successfully adapting to difficult or challenging life experiences, especially through mental, emotional, and behavioral flexibility and adjustment to external and internal demands. A number of factors contribute to how well people adapt to adversities, predominant among them (a) the ways in which individuals view and engage with the world, (b) the availability and quality of social resources, and (c) specific coping strategies. Psychological research demonstrates that the resources and skills associated with more positive adaptation (i.e., greater resilience) can be cultivated and practiced. [1]

Handling life's difficulties includes several key components, such as how you behave after getting deeply disturbed by adversity, whether you get angry with yourself or with the source of the adversity, and whether you persist in your enterprise despite everyone telling you to just give up and do something else.

Being mentally resilient doesn't mean you won't experience sadness, frustration, embarrassment, anger, anxiety, guilt, or any other negative emotion for that matter. You will continue to experience them. You see, just like trying to stop your brain from entering the fight-or-flight mode, you can't prevent yourself from experiencing emotions. They are a natural process carried out by your gray matter. Emotions have a purpose in life. How you analyze the events and circumstances that influence those emotions, how you respond to them, and whether you can bounce back will determine your mental resilience levels. That's because your resilience is a by-product of your feelings, behaviors, and thoughts. Your resilience, then, is your "ability to persevere and adapt when things go awry."[2]

Many psychologists say that the degree of resilience we have in adulthood is influenced in large part by our childhood experiences and upbringing. The factors that make up that influence include the weight of the newborn baby, the socio-economic background of the parents, whether there was physical or emotional abuse, and whether the parents got a divorce or not. Fortunately, the thinking style adopted in childhood that leads to lower mental resilience when we become adults can be changed. One crucial thing to keep in mind while you read this book is that you can change your behaviors, thoughts, and feelings. These three things might well be the only things we have real control over in this life.

A very important psychologist, Alber Ellis, the considered grandfather of cognitive behavioral therapy (CBT) and the creator of rational emotive behavior therapy (REBT), seemed to think that the experiences of our childhood were secondary to our resilience. Actually, let me rephrase that—he believed they had no bearing on how you handle tough situations. Why is that? Because he was a proponent of the idea that we are responsible for the way we feel during difficult situations. Much like the stoics before him have explained, Ellis stated that how we interpret the situations we experience is responsible for our behavior, feelings, and thoughts, not the situations per se.

I have mentioned behaviors, feelings, and thoughts a couple of times already. Why do I keep repeating myself? If you haven't realized yet, it's because those three things are very important. Aaron Beck, the father of cognitive behavioral therapy (CBT), came up with the concept of the cognitive triad, or negative triad. It describes the influence of three key factors in a patient's thought pattern of suffering from depression. They are:

- the self,
- the world/environment,
- the future.

They each influence the other. For example, a depressed patient may think that everything they do is bound to fail (the self), leading them to think no one respects or values them because they are always failing (the world). As a result, they might imagine a bleak future where they end up living under a bridge and eating cat food for the rest of their lives (the future).

The cognitive triangle, based on Beck's cognitive triad[3], swaps the self, the world/environment, and the future for thoughts, behaviors, and feelings. In other words:

- **Thoughts** influence behaviors and feelings.
- **Feelings** influence thoughts and behaviors.
- **Behaviors** influence thoughts and feelings.

The cognitive triangle is used by therapists to highlight irrational thinking in their patients. The patients don't have to suffer exclusively from depression to benefit from the triangle; the tool is useful for all kinds of negative thinking patterns. Although Albert Ellis didn't use Beck's cognitive triad (or the cognitive triangle) in his REBT, knowing about and understanding it will help you put things in perspective and support you in your journey to increased mental resilience.

For example, remember I mentioned that our interpretation of a situation is the source of our misery, not the event itself? The cognitive triangle can help you see that more clearly. Here's an example: remember Steve Irwin, the Australian zookeeper, conservationist and TV presenter, also known as "The Crocodile Hunter?" He was passionate about all kinds of animals, not only crocodiles (funnily enough, he wasn't comfortable around parrots). Some of the animals he introduced on his shows were very dangerous, like venomous snakes and spiders. Others, like the gentle blue-tongue skink, were harmless (although most people wouldn't touch them with a ten-foot pole). How was it possible that, for him, being able to interact with such animals was an awesome experience? And why is it that, for so many people, it's a gut-wrenching ordeal? There's one explanation—it's all down to how your brain interprets the situation. Being bitten by a snake on live TV was not a source of mental agony for the late Mr. Irwin. The same thing can be said for normal situations we face in our daily lives. Some situations may make you squirm, while other people may feel something completely different—the idea of public speaking might make some people squirm with anxiety; someone else might find it exhilarating and energizing. A job interview might feel overwhelming for one and an exciting opportunity for another.

Becoming mentally resilient has many benefits. Among them are:

- **Stress management**: When we're more resilient, we are better able to handle situations that affect us more than usual, such as everyday pressure. Since unhealthy stress affects nearly every system in your body, being more resilient allows you to lessen its impact not only on your body but also on your feelings, behaviors, and thoughts.

- **Negative emotions management**: when our emotions are out of control, they can influence our actions when facing stressful situations and the thoughts that ensue. You can decrease that influence with the techniques provided in this book. (Remember, there's no way to stop the brain from creating emotions.)

- **Tolerance for failure**: when we keep our emotions/feelings, thoughts, or behaviors in check, we tend to increase our resilience. The more resilience we have, the better we will manage the three items in our cognitive triangle in a positive feedback loop. However, that loop is not perfect, nor does it happen indefinitely.

We all have our ups and downs. In one moment, everything is smooth sailing; the next, nothing seems to go our way. Such is the burden of life. Resilience provides a way for you to accept that fact and deal with the aftermath of a failure. It will also indirectly help you to learn from the mistakes you make.

- **Increased tolerance for discomfort and the need for immediate gratification**: let's be real, life isn't easy. There will be countless moments of discomfort, adversities, and insurmountable obstacles. When faced with these, our instinct (whether biological or psychological) is to cut our losses and go on with our lives. REBT, CBT, and other cognitive therapies help us to hang in there (as long as doing so helps us fulfill our goals) and avoid the immediate desire to gratify ourselves to the detriment of future gains.

Now is a good time to stop and talk about the source of irrationality.

The Biology of Irrationality

Humans are complex, and sometimes, they are difficult to understand. What part of our normal behaviors are created by our environments? What about our upbringing? Which are a product of our DNA? And further still, which are a product of our eccentricity?

Albert Ellis, in his book *How to Stubbornly Refuse to Make Yourself Miserable About Anything—yes, Anything!*[4], states that the irrational behaviors, thoughts, and feelings that we are often plagued with are biological in origin, i.e., genetic and/or congenital. You could say that they're part of our human nature. Our irrational behaviors, thoughts, and feelings are, therefore, the easiest and most natural ones to "perform" when confronted with adversities, and many times, we do them against our better judgment, advice from loved ones, or societal customs. He states that practically everyone acts irrationally, although some more than others. He also adds that although it's possible to change said irrational behaviors, feelings, and thoughts, it's not always possible to eliminate them completely. This could explain why so many people have problems getting rid of their negative thoughts or revert to their old ways after going through psychotherapy (I am an example). Some people apply the concepts in this book for a certain period and go through a positive transformation, only to stop practicing the techniques due to laziness, experiencing a hectic period in their lives, or some other reasons. It is then that they revert to their old habits.

What follows are examples of irrationalities. The list is just for your reference; it's not even close to being exhaustive. Please understand that not all irrational behavior presents a complete disadvantage to our survival, although it can be said to be very foolish and a disadvantage to our happiness.

- Personalization
- Overgeneralization
- Arbitrary inference (jumping to conclusions)
- Minimization and magnification
- Selective abstraction (mental filter)
- Absolutistic dichotomous thinking (all-or-nothing)
- Perfectionism
- Prejudice (racial, political, religious, social, sexual, etc)
- Addiction (alcohol, cigarettes, food, medicine, illicit drugs, etc.)
- Procrastination
- Over-reliance on should/must statements
- The need to have superiority over others
- Depression

- Excessive hostility and rage
- Extreme self-pity
- Extreme nationalism and patriotism
- Approval-seeking behaviors
- Excessive belief in pseudo-scientific fields (astrology, climate-change denial, chromotherapy, fad diets, etc.)
- Belief that science is the solution to all problems faced by humankind
- Magic-related beliefs (sorcery, black magic, necromancy, etc.)

Don't worry if you recognize some of the items above in your own life. Who can say they never have or never will display any of the irrationalities from that short list? Just know that it's possible to manage most of the issues mentioned. Some are so difficult they may require the help of professionals. Consult your local mental health care provider for help.

Sources of Disturbance

REBT poses two questions to help you become aware of negative thoughts so you can start changing them. The first question is rather simple: ask yourself, "How do I feel?" When you feel bad, it's easy to recognize what you feel at any moment. Other times, you have to take a long, hard look deep inside and stop trying to fool yourself. After you have an idea of what kind of feelings you are experiencing, ask yourself the second question: "How healthy are these feelings?"

Unlike other behavior therapies, Ellis's REBT separates healthy feelings from unhealthy feelings. REBT considers strong feelings of concern, sadness, and irritation healthy because they allow you to work on changing them. Feelings like rage, depression, and anxiety are, most times, unhealthy. Your unrealistic expectations that bad things should never happen to you are the ones responsible for you feeling like that. They affect your coping mechanisms so negatively that they may stall your life's progress. Remember this one important fact about us human beings: we are the ones who create healthy and unhealthy feelings when confronted with obstacles.

Now, things get a bit complicated because your feelings aren't always neatly defined. Sometimes, you'll feel both healthy and unhealthy feelings at the same time. Starting with unhealthy feelings, the keyword to define them is *must*. In the previous section, I presented a few examples of irrationalities that influence our behaviors and feelings. One of them was "over-reliance on should/must statements."[5] That item is a big one. It's central to Albert Ellis's REBT. He even gave it a funny-looking, giggle-inducing name: *musturbation*. What does that even mean? Things will become clearer in a moment, so read on.

There are two main kinds of beliefs that lead to our healthy and unhealthy behaviors: rational beliefs and irrational beliefs. Rational beliefs allow you to make decisions in life that lead to more things that make you happy and fulfill your wants and desires and less of the things you want to avoid. They are characterized by thoughts (and behaviors and feelings) that are either cool or warm.

Cool thoughts, behaviors, and feelings describe life events as they happen. You feel calm and don't make rash decisions. Here's an example: imagine you are stuck in traffic at night trying to get home during a thunderstorm, and the streets are getting flooded at an alarmingly fast rate. You arrive at a crossroads, but it seems the water is deep, and there may be a strong current, but since it's dark, you can't see properly. Some drivers try their luck and cross successfully. Your turn to cross finally arrives. You don't really know what the best way to do it is: should you accelerate and try to cross it at high speed, or should you take it slowly? Should you give up and wait? A cool thought would be: *There's a lot of water, and there may be a strong current*. This thought is cool because it allows you to see what is happening, but you don't make a judgment or decision that you may regret later.

Here's another example: you are giving a presentation on a project proposal to your boss, your potential client, and some team members. You can see that both the client and your boss changed their facial expressions from resting to scowling, just as you revealed the main point of your presentation. Your cool thought is *that John and the client are frowning; they may not accept my proposal.* That's it. You're not rating or evaluating the situation; you're just describing what is happening to yourself.

Warm thoughts, on the other hand, are thoughts that include your wishes and desires, as well as your likes and dislikes. You are effectively evaluating the situation, rating it on a personal scale, and knowing whether it helps you with your goals or hinders them. Going back to the car situation above: if you risk going through the water, you might get home on time to tuck your kids into bed and read a story for them (your goal is to get home quickly), or you might get stuck in the water (and have to pay to fix all the water damage to the engine block and upholstery), or even worse, get dragged away by the water into a storm drain. Another alternative is to wait for the storm and the waters to abate.

Your warm thoughts could be: *I'd love to get home tonight and tuck in my kids and read their favorite book. I wish I could avoid this route. I don't like being stuck here, waiting for the rain to stop. Unfortunately, this is the only way to get home.*

How about the presentation example? *Hmm, John and the client are frowning. I don't like the look on their faces. Maybe they don't like my proposal. I wish they would stop doing that and just wait until the end of my presentation. That would be grand.*

The interesting thing about warm thoughts is that they're not dogma. They aren't rigid. They aren't certainties either. They're just probabilities. Look at the examples above. In the first one, there is a chance you might not be able to get home at the time you wanted. You would then add: *I might not be able to see my kids tonight* to your warm thoughts. In the second example, you might think: *the client might not approve this proposal. I'd love it if they did, but it's the client's choice. I don't have to get it approved since we are already working on five other projects with such a small team. It would be great for my career, though.*

The other type of belief concerns **irrational beliefs**. Unlike rational beliefs, they make you feel, behave, and think unhealthily. They are ineffective modes of operation because they mess up your goals. They prevent you from getting more of what you want and shove things you don't want down your throat. They might start with cool and warm thoughts devoid of evaluation, but they tend to devolve into **hot thoughts**. "What are those?" you may ask. **Hot thoughts** are instances where you rate situations on your personal scale and evaluate them, often negatively. And to make matters worse, they are dogmatic, absolutist, and commanding!

What would a **hot thought** look like in the examples I gave above? In the car situation, they would sound like this: *I have to get home and see my kids before they sleep! I must cross this water. I don't care that it's dark. I'm not worried about expensive car repairs. It's unacceptable for a parent to not spend more time with their children. If I don't get home soon, my kids will hate me. They won't call when they grow up and have their own families. I can't stand this thought. It's imperative that I be more present in their lives!*

In the presentation example, a **hot thought** would look like this: *I can't believe they're making that face. I'm not even halfway through my first agenda item, and they already hate it! That's not good, not good at all. That probably means I won't get this project. No! I must get this project at all costs! If I don't, it'll prove that I'm incompetent; I'll feel like a failure, my career will derail, I'll lose my job, and I'll have to move in with my parents.*

These examples may sound a bit extreme, far-fetched, or unrealistic. However, all people can have **hot thoughts** or imagine a bleak future. As I explained before, everyone can come up with negative thoughts regardless of whether them having a mental health condition or not. The degree to which these thoughts can be bad, of course, will change from person to person.

Another caveat is warranted now: not every single irrational thought that goes through your head will upset your emotional balance. That is clear when you watch in disbelief when a friend or family member makes biased, racist, or downright shocking remarks about groups of people they don't like without them batting an eye. Or when you believe that all men are evil and cheaters (if you're a woman) or that all women are crazy and cheaters (if you're a man). These examples of irrational thoughts may or may not lead you (or your friends or family members) to feel upset emotionally.

When you have rigid and commanding irrational thoughts, you are setting yourself up for failure when trying to achieve your goals or maintain a semblance of emotional balance. What can you expect to happen when you constantly think, "I must do well in this test, or..." "I have to woo this person right now, or else..." "I need to be respected by everyone, or..." but then, none of these things go the way you wanted?

This leads us to one of the most important concepts of **REBT**: the notion of **musturbation**. This word is used to explain the rigid, irrational beliefs that many people have about themselves, others, and the world around them. Expect these same people to feel miserable when blindly following those precepts and not realizing why they feel like that—or why other people stop associating with them. When your brain devises statements containing the words *must*, *should*, *have to*, *need to*, or *ought to*, in an absolute, no-other-possibility context, you're likely suffering from **musturbation**.

Albert Ellis originally came up with twelve basic patterns of irrational beliefs. However, he later came to condense them into three main *musts* that lead to a disturbed emotional state. They are:

- **I must perform well/be accepted, and win the**

approval of my peers and important people. If I don't, then I must be incompetent/inadequate.

- **You must treat me in a fair, kind, and respectful manner at all times.** You must not treat me badly nor frustrate or hinder my progress whatsoever. If you do, then you're a bad, immoral, and lousy person.
- **Life circumstances must be ideal for my well-being, safety, goals, and happiness.** They must allow all the things that I want in life, but they must not allow things that I hate into my life. Otherwise, I'll never be happy, and life will become intolerable.

You may have noticed that the three items above are fairly rigid. They don't allow for anything else besides *musts* to be manifested. They are a stark contrast to cool or warm thoughts, which only state preferences rather than demands. You are probably well aware that life is a box full of surprises. Some of them are going to be pleasant, others not so much. There are countless things outside of our control. Letting **hot thoughts** (and consequently *musturbation*) run amok is bound to frustrate your expectations.

A better alternative to **hot thoughts** is to let go of the concept that things must go your way and that you shouldn't get upset by things you experience in life. It's all right to experience sadness, frustration, and other healthy negative feelings. They are your friends. You can't let them become more than that; you can't allow them to become unhealthy ones. The methods to achieve this will be discussed in Chapters 2 and 3.

But how do we differentiate a healthy feeling from an unhealthy one?

One way to distinguish your healthy feelings from unhealthy ones is to look for cool, warm, and **hot thoughts**. The healthy ones can be either cool or warm, while the unhealthy ones are characterized by hot thoughts.

Healthy feelings, whether negative or positive, are realistic and appropriate for the context in which they are expressed. **Unhealthy feelings** are not reasonable. They affect your behaviors and thoughts in a negative way. **Unhealthy feelings** are characterized by demands. Look for the *shoulds* and the *musts*. If you find any rigid demands there, then the feelings are unhealthy.

Think of the examples I gave earlier. It would be nice to cross that water during the storm to get home and read a story to your kids before bed. You don't have to, though. Why? Is it worth dying and leaving your spouse all alone to take care of your kids? Sounds a bit too dramatic? Maybe. That section of the road could crumble under the weight of your vehicle and get swept into a river. Or there's a live power line that got knocked over or debris that might immobilize your car in the middle of the flooded section. The risks are just not worth it. There are other ways to be a great parent than having to tuck in your kids every night.

Wouldn't it be wonderful if you got that contract after the presentation? It's natural to wish for. But you don't *have to*. If you don't get it, that's okay, too. You're allowed to feel disappointed. It's not the end of the world, and you will have other opportunities to pitch to new potential clients. This one outcome doesn't reflect your competency, the skills you bring to the company, or your value as a human being.

Now that we have discussed the sources of disturbance, let's go ahead and talk about a type of psychotherapy called **REBT**.

What is REBT?

Rational emotive behavior therapy (REBT) was created by Albert Ellis in the mid-1950s[6]. Before that, he practiced Freudian psychoanalysis for six years before creating what he called at the time **rational therapy (RT)**. He believed that helping clients understand the origins of what was bothering them via psychoanalysis was not enough as "they hardly did a damn thing to change."[7] He renamed his techniques to *rational emotive therapy* in 1959, then again to *rational emotive behavior therapy* (REBT) in 1993. **REBT** is considered the precursor to Aaron Beck's cognitive behavioral therapy (CBT)[8].

Ellis based core aspects of his techniques on the teachings of famous stoic philosophers such as Marcus Aurelius, Seneca, and Epictetus. Some early Asian philosophies' ideas, such as Confucianism and Buddhism, were also identified in **REBT**.

There are three main philosophies behind REBT:

- being aware of your irrational beliefs,
- disrupting them,
- arriving at new, rational coping philosophies.

The three main coping philosophies are:

- Unconditional Self-Acceptance (USA),
- Unconditional Other-Acceptance (UOA),
- Unconditional Life-Acceptance (ULA).

Unconditional self-acceptance highlights the importance of accepting one's self rather than possessing **conditional self-esteem (CSE)**. To Ellis, self-esteem is the bane of people's mental health; it's completely conditional and, at best, temporary: "If I do this, then this person will love me," "If I behave like that, then my peers will accept me," "When I say these things, people think I'm intelligent and articulate, and I feel great," etc.

To accept yourself unconditionally, evaluate your actions, feelings, and thoughts as good or effective when they aid you in your quest to survive and be happy. Alternatively, you can rate them as ineffective or bad should you find they're preventing you from achieving your goals of survival and happiness. Don't evaluate yourself; only consider your thoughts, behaviors, and feelings. This allows you to accept and respect yourself, including your mistakes, past, and uniqueness. You accept whether or not you perform well, and you accept whether or not people approve of your behavior and who you are.

The second coping philosophy is unconditional other-acceptance. Like **USA**, this teaches you to learn to evaluate other people's thoughts, feelings, and behaviors as good or bad. That evaluation depends on your social standards and the general social standards of your culture. You don't rate them just as you wouldn't rate yourself as good or bad; only deeds, thoughts, and feelings matter. You don't have to accept everything they do or every part of their personalities.

Some people do shitty things from time to time, but that doesn't necessarily make them evil or unlovable. After all, they are human beings and, therefore, far from perfect. Just like you, they make mistakes and do good and bad things. Tolerance is key, but make no mistake, that doesn't give you carte blanche to do whatever you want, nor should you accept acts that violate another person or sentient animal's physical and mental welfare (you wouldn't accept someone defending the torture and killing of puppies or kittens as part of their culture, would you?).

The third philosophy is **unconditional life-acceptance (ULA)**. As the name states, **ULA** goes against one of Ellis' main sources of misery, which is that "Life circumstances must be easy." When life isn't easy, when your wishes and desires are not immediately fulfilled, you probably get upset, maybe throw a tantrum, and curse everything and everyone. **ULA** allows you to accept the conditions of life the way they are: full of frustration, hardships, injustice, corruption, poverty, disease, and death, but also full of memorable moments of happiness, joy, opportunities, love, friendship, and passion. This is not about giving up on the current situation of your life or the world; it's about acknowledging the state your life and the world are in and being aware of what you can change and what you can't. If you often shake your fists at the sky, demanding that the world or your life conditions be different, then incorporating **ULA** into your life will be a challenge. Here, the objective is to evaluate life's conditions, moments, and hardships as good or bad. This evaluation must also be per your personal standards and goals, as well as your community's standards and social mores. The important thing to keep in mind is to not evaluate your life itself as bad or good.

Let's stop here; I have to make a very important point: adopting these three main philosophies doesn't mean you will certainly and unconditionally be happy, all your problems will vanish, and the world will be full of rainbows and unicorns, far from it. These philosophies are coping strategies, not pills you swallow, and everything turns out fine. Changing healthy thoughts, feelings, and behaviors into unhealthy ones is easy. Most of us have been doing it since early childhood. Nevertheless, it takes a lot of effort to change this pattern.

How Can You Be More Resilient?

For starters, adopting Ellis' three coping philosophies is a very good start. These philosophies help you reduce issues with the cognitive triangle of thoughts, behaviors, and feelings.

What else can you do, then? Start by paying attention to your tendencies of applying *shoulds* and *musts* to the situations you face in life. Look at your irrational beliefs and see how they affect your thoughts and feelings. When you become aware of those tendencies and irrational beliefs, the next step is to dispute them. One of the best ways of doing so is using a technique called **ABC** (or its variants, such as the **ABCDE** and the **ABCDEF**). Another useful technique is the scientific method. Both of these techniques will be discussed in Chapters 2 and 3.

Here's a piece of advice courtesy of Albert Ellis that has helped me a lot in my journey to become more resilient. I recommend that you tell yourself every morning: "I will not should on myself today."[9]

Key Takeaways

- Resilience is the ability to handle your emotions when something disturbs your inner peace.
- Our interpretation of a situation is the source of our misery, not the event itself.
- Rational beliefs, thoughts, and behaviors can be cool or warm. **Cool thoughts** are descriptions of life events as they happen. Warm thoughts include your wishes and desires as well as your likes and dislikes.
- **Irrational beliefs** make you feel (and behave and think) unhealthy and usually turn into **hot thoughts**, instances of negative thoughts that are dogmatic, absolutist, and commanding.
- **Musturbation** is the main source of disturbance and involves three categories: me, others, and the world.
- **REBT** has three main philosophies: being aware of your irrational beliefs, disrupting them, and arriving at new, rational coping philosophies. They are useful in countering the above three categories of musturbation.
- **REBT** has three coping mechanisms: **unconditional self-acceptance (USA)**, **unconditional other-acceptance (UOA)**, and **unconditional life-acceptance (ULA).**

Now that you know more about irrational beliefs, thoughts, and behaviors, let's discuss the first technique, the **ABC model.**

---

1. American Psychological Association, *APA Dictionary of Psychology*, 2nd ed. (Washington, DC: American Psychological Association, 2015), 862.
2. Karen Reivich and Andrew Shatté, *The Resilience Factor: 7 Keys to Finding Your Inner Strength and Overcoming Life's Hurdles* (New York: Broadway Books, 2002), 45.

3. Beck, Aaron T. *Cognitive Therapy and the Emotional Disorders*. (New York: International Universities Press, 1976).

4. Albert Ellis, *How to Stubbornly Refuse to Make Yourself Miserable About Anything—Yes, Anything!* (New York, NJ: Kensington Publishing Corp., 2006).

5. Ellis, *How to Stubbornly Refuse to Make Yourself Miserable.*

6. Ellis, Albert. "Rational Psychotherapy and Individual Psychology," presented at the American Psychological Association Conference, 1956.

7. Ellis, Albert. 2001. "The Prince of Reason." Interview by Robert Epstein. Psychology Today. January 2001. https://www.psychologytoday.com/gb/articles/200101/the-prince-reason.

8. David, Daniel, Cotet C, Matu S, Mogoase C, Stefan S. "50 Years of Rational-Emotive and Cognitive-Behavioral Therapy: A Systematic Review and Meta-Analysis." *J Clin Psychol*. 2018.

9. Ellis, Albert. 2001. "The Prince of Reason." Interview by Robert Epstein. *Psychology Today*. January 2001. https://www.psychologytoday.com/gb/articles/200101/the-prince-reason.

Chapter Two

Know Yourself

Knowing yourself is the beginning of all wisdom.
—Aristotle, ancient Greek philosopher and scientist

You may have heard about a specific type of psychotherapy called insight-oriented therapy, which aims to increase the patient's understanding of events, both past and present, and the correlation those events have on emotions, relationships, and even psychological symptoms. I have done this type of therapy for several years, mostly during my university years. Unfortunately, I could not make effective changes even after learning more about my issues, a concern that Albert Ellis highlighted in interviews several times. Please note that I'm not saying this type of therapy is ineffective, but that other forms of therapy may be more efficient for some people.

Despite not being able to make much progress personally, I can't deny the fact that countless patients do get better with insight-oriented psychotherapy. Even Ellis himself, who had lost faith in psychoanalysis and started REBT in the mid-1950s, must have recognized that insight is important. After all, he even created the **ABC model**—used in **CBT** and **REBT**—for that matter. So, what is the **ABC model**? Put simply, it's a tool designed to give you insight into your negative thoughts and emotions. Only then can you work on changing them.

In this chapter, we will talk about important topics and tools that will help you make progress on the road to better resilience. We'll cover the **ABC model**, unhelpful thinking patterns, and how to handle these negative thoughts and **iceberg beliefs**. All right, let's start by learning our ABCs.

The ABC Model

The first thing we need to do to help us get a grip on our emotions is to learn how to use the **ABC model** (there is a variant, unsurprisingly called the ABCDE model, which we'll discuss in Chapter 3). The **ABC model** was invented by Dr. Albert Ellis[1] and is used in several different therapies for many different problems, such as depression and cognitive distortions (aka unhelpful thinking patterns). This model allows you to see how thoughts or beliefs negatively impact your feelings and your behaviors and that the events themselves are not the source of your disturbance. Let's break down the **ABC model** into its components first.

(A) Adversity

The first item of this model is the letter **A**, short for **Adversity**. It's the event or situation that triggers a reaction—often a negative one—after being processed by your cortex and going through your beliefs "filter." It doesn't have to be a big event like a natural disaster, the death of a loved one, or a severe stock market crash (and, with it, your retirement fund). The adversity could be smaller in scale, such as a fight with your significant other, the lack of help from family members in household chores, getting rejected by a potential romantic partner or making a mistake at work.

Generally speaking, we handle the majority of the events in our lives efficiently without creating any further problems. Watch out for the button-push adversities, though. Our interpretation of these events can really rattle one's cage, shake us to the core, ruffle our feathers, well, you get the idea. How so? By influencing what we feel and how we behave following the event in question (which, in turn, lowers our resilience). Allow me to sound like a broken record and say it again: our interpretation of events—the **B** in the **ABC model**—is responsible for these feelings and behaviors—the **C** in the **ABC**; more on that later. That means the same event that makes you terrified might make someone else excited and happy. At any rate, our problem-solving skills and ability to think clearly are likely to take a hit; our decision-making skills may also decline in performance when we are faced with adversity.

Here is a short list of situations that commonly aggravate people:

- Dealing with feelings of anxiety, shame/guilt, anger, embarrassment, sadness.
- Dealing with conflicts (with superiors, coworkers, friends, family).
- Dealing with success and failure.
- Dealing with heavy workloads, tight schedules and deadlines, and new responsibilities.
- Dealing with issues with work-life balance.
- Dealing with both positive and negative feedback.
- Dealing with and adapting to unexpected changes.

Some people will experience more of the above situations in life than other people around them. Some of the situations above will aggravate them more than the other situations. Some situations will have a common emotional response, such as anxiety when dealing with changes in the work and family spheres.

(B) Belief

The second item of this model, B, means **Belief**. When something unpleasant happens to you, your brain will come up with thoughts that reflect your beliefs. Consider these thoughts and beliefs the things you tell yourself immediately as adversity pushes your buttons. You aren't always aware of these beliefs. What you do and feel will directly correlate to your thoughts/beliefs. If you possess healthy, rational beliefs, then your actions and emotions will allow you to handle the present adversity effectively, as well as help you achieve your goals. On the other hand, if your beliefs are unhealthy and irrational, your ability to handle difficulties appropriately will be greatly diminished.

Karen Reivich and Andrew Shatté, authors of the book *The Resilience Factor*[2], determined that there are two main categories of beliefs that assist us in increasing our mental resilience: causal beliefs (or "why beliefs") and implication beliefs (or "what-next beliefs"). Causal beliefs are probably evolutionary consequences of our thinking abilities. Looking for why bad things happen to us aids our efforts of searching for solutions so we can achieve our goals and may even help avoid similar situations in the future. Martin Seligman, a psychologist famous for the concept of learned helplessness, together with other researchers, discovered that the answers to this type of questioning slot into three sub-categories: personal (me-not me), permanent (always-not always) and pervasive (everything-not everything). Our response to adversity tends to follow the same patterns most of the time: do we blame ourselves or others? Is the problem a temporary one or a permanent one? Will it affect everything in life or just this one issue? Think about your own past dealing with adversities: what patterns can you see when asking yourself, "Why?"

Implication beliefs (aka "what-next") are focused on the future or, more specifically, what will happen next. Although this belief clearly has its advantages, it often results in incorrect assessments and anxiety, which ultimately deteriorates our mental resilience.

The two categories above are not the only ones we use in daily life. Other categories exist, such as evaluation (rating events in life as good or bad) and narration (explaining the event to yourself without looking for causes or making predictions for the future). There's even a mixture of all the above, although most people have a primary explanatory style.

(C) Consequences

The letter C, **Consequences**, represents what you feel and what you do according to your beliefs when facing adversity. Many people think that Adversities cause **Consequences**. As you probably already know from reading this book (and I'll keep repeating it because it's a major point in improving your resilience), A does not cause C. B causes C. This discovery was made long before Albert Ellis' REBT. The stoics, such as Epictetus, in his work *The Enchiridion*, pointed this concept out more than 2,000 years ago — "Men are disturbed not by things, but by the views which they take of them."[3] Even Shakespeare represented that concept in his magnum opus, *Hamlet* (Act II, Scene II): "Why, then, 'tis none to you, for there is nothing either good or bad, but thinking makes it so."

I already mentioned in Chapter 1 that sources of disturbance come from our rational and irrational beliefs. Rational beliefs include cool or warm thoughts (the former mainly describes what is going on; the latter evaluates the situation while expressing your wishes and preferences). Irrational beliefs include cool and warm thoughts as well as **hot thoughts**—dogmatic, commanding thoughts full of shoulds and musts.

Certain universal **Belief–Consequence** pairs help us predict how people (and ourselves) could respond during difficult events. Look at the table below:

	Belief	Consequence
1	Future threat	Anxiety
2	Comparison to others in a negative light	Embarrassment/shame
3	Infringements on others' rights	Guilt
4	Infringements on your rights	Anger
5	Grief and loss (e.g. a loved one, self-esteem)	Sadness/depression

Can you think of examples of the above? I'm willing to bet you have experienced all five of the pairs presented above at one point or another in your life. Let's discuss the pairs briefly:

- **Potential threats in the future (real or imagined) lead to anxiety**. Anxiety may lead to fear and panic attacks, depending on certain factors (such as panic disorder diagnosis). And before you protest, claiming to not have any anxiety, know that it's a normal process of the brain. For some people, it's just a blip in their "radar" that shows up from time to time, while for others, it can be paralyzing, effectively confining them to their own homes. The amygdala (we have one on each side of the brain) is responsible, in large part, for the fear, panic, and all the other physical sensations we feel when we are in danger. When it overreacts, it can hijack our bodies even when the reason for the fear we feel is not there (agoraphobia and obsessive-compulsive disorder are two examples). Excessive anxiety, then, is understood as an obstacle to a rational, healthy lifestyle. Read the excellent book *Rewire Your Anxious Brain: How to Use the Neuroscience of Fear to End Anxiety, Panic, and Worry*[4] for more information on how the amygdala works.

- **Comparison to others in a negative light leads to embarrassment/shame**. That goes for those situations when we compare ourselves to other people, too, not just when others comment how Tom's presentations are so much fun compared to ours. That means you don't need an audience to feel embarrassment or shame. You only need to act, think, or feel in a way that goes against your standards. Need examples? Here you go: Imagine your mother making fun of your choice to study philosophy, art history, or theology to everyone at the table at your brother's wedding celebration. To add insult to injury, she might even mention your cousin, who is a successful plastic surgeon. How would you feel in that situation?Here's another one: you sent your boss an email complaining about a coworker's attitude during a meeting with a client. However, you later realized you were not being fair in your assessment of the situation and remembered a time when that same coworker defended you when another client made a bogus complaint about you. How would you feel? Depending on your beliefs and values, you might feel shame. And how would you feel if that coworker pointed out, during a team meeting, not only your lack of fairness but also your blunders from the last couple of projects?

- **Infringement of other people's rights leads to guilt.** This means the infringements you committed against others. According to Psychology Today, there are five main reasons for guilt: guilt for something you did, guilt for something you didn't do but want to, guilt for something you think you did, guilt that you didn't do enough to help someone, and guilt that you're doing better than someone else (Whitbourne, "Guide to guilt")[5]. Two types of offense can also generate guilt: **commitments** and **self-regulation**. The former relates to ignoring friends and family and cheating on your romantic partner, for example. The latter refers to things such as excessive drinking and eating, spending too much money, procrastination, and lack of exercise. Guilt is a useful emotion that allows us to live in harmony. Otherwise, we would have far more people displaying sociopathic behavior. It helps us stop with the Netflix binge sessions and get to the gym. It allows us to make amends when we hurt others. Shame may also make an appearance when you realize that you've just hurt others and may think that such action makes you a very bad person.

- **Infringements on your rights lead to anger or other related emotions like rage, wrath, fury, annoyance, and irritation**. It usually happens when you believe someone is trying to harm you and they are doing it on purpose. There are a few ways we believe a person is trying to harm us: by unfairly treating us, preventing us from reaching our goals or making a disparaging remark that hurts our self-esteem. When we face situations like these, we tend to ask ourselves why that's happening to us right before anger consumes us. Let's say you were looking forward to enjoying that last slice of leftover cake from your birthday party. When you get home from school or work, you open the fridge only to see that someone else has already eaten it. Your spouse/child/family member is the only one in the house, so you immediately conclude that they ate the cake before you arrived. Why did they do that when they knew you wanted it? You might think that the reason is because they are selfish, ungrateful people who enjoy seeing you upset. Then anger washes over you, and you slam the fridge door shut and stomp your feet on your way to the living room. You feel your rights have been effectively violated.

- **Grief and loss lead to sadness and depression**. When we lose someone dear to us, we become sad. The same feeling arises when we lose our jobs or a romantic relationship. Sometimes, we may even get depressed after a loss. It doesn't have to be someone or something, either (like losing a family heirloom). It can be something abstract as well. When you discover that a friend or family member posted photos online of a party but didn't invite you, how do you feel? How do you feel when someone declines your invitation for a second date or simply ghosts you? The answer tends to be feelings of sadness or depression. Feeling sad per se is not always a bad thing. It's a normal emotion. When your sadness becomes too much and turns into depression, you'll probably waste a lot of time focusing on your depression to the detriment of other aspects of life. Don't let that happen.

How to Use This Knowledge

How can we use the knowledge we just acquired to help us with mental resilience? Many times in life, our emotions won't be as clear cut as shown in the table from the previous section. It's important to try to separate each emotion so you can get a clear picture of what's happening and work on each.

The first step is to chart your adversities following the **ABC model**. Here, you need to focus on the A and describe it in a clear, impartial way. Imagine you're a journalist covering a story. It's your job to identify the what, who, when, and where. Don't worry about the why right now; that will come in the third step. For example, imagine your company sent an ominous email to everyone implying that it needs to restructure to remain profitable. It doesn't mention which departments are getting affected, but it does mention that everyone needs to go through an interview starting the following week. From the email alone, you know the who (everyone, including you), the what (an interview to assess who will get the chop), when (starting the following week), and where (at the company); that's it. Don't include any extra information, like your interpretation of the event. You can put everything together in a sentence like this: "I will have an interview next week at the office to assess whether I'll remain in the company or not."

The second step is to work on the event's **consequences**, the **C**s. We're skipping the Bs now because we tend to react to situations that push our buttons without being fully aware of the beliefs that drive them. You might only realize the justifications of your actions and emotions after. Your objective, then, will be to slow things down and break this cycle as best as you can. You can start by writing down your feelings and behaviors. What did you feel at the moment the issue arose? How would you classify those emotions? Are they mild, moderate, or intense? What was the first thing you did? Using the company-wide email situation, let's say you felt intense anxiety and moderate irritation. You immediately went over to your team leader to ask for details, but she was clearly annoyed by your questioning and made a snide comment that left you scratching your head. So you discreetly started looking for a new job on your smartphone and half-heartedly worked on some tasks for a project with a looming deadline for the rest of the day.

Now, it's time to start the third step. The objective is to identify the **beliefs (B)** that set off the **consequences (C)** of the **adversity (A)**. Be honest with yourself; don't filter those thoughts through a politically correct lens. Let the raw version of those beliefs come to the surface. What were you thinking that made you feel and behave the way you did in **C**? In the previous example, the belief that you will lose your job and get into debt will lead to a strenuous relationship with your spouse; they will lose their faith in you, ask for a divorce, and you'll be lonely for the rest of your life; you fear you will die as a homeless under a bridge. This seems a little far-fetched, but our brains can surprise us sometimes. This is an example of a universal future threat that leads to anxiety. The resulting behavior is to immediately search for a new job online. The other emotion you felt was irritation, which originated from the perception that your rights were being violated by the company. You felt irritated by the fact that the company didn't care about its workers and would rather fire the employees as a first measure. Their families and wellbeing be damned. So, what did you do? You "worked" on one of the projects that had an imminent deadline, but only in a lazy manner.

Here's a table with the example we discussed above:

(A) Adversity	I will have an interview next week at the office to assess whether I'll remain in the company or not.
(B) Beliefs	1. I'll lose my job and will die alone under a bridge. 2. Company doesn't care about its workers.
(C) Consequences	1. Intense anxiety. Started looking for a new job. 2. Moderate irritation. Pretended to work on a project.

While you're working on your **ABC**s, look for universal beliefs such as infringement of your rights, future threats, grief and loss. Are there more what-next beliefs compared to why beliefs? Do you see any should/must statements hiding somewhere? Each belief should connect with its consequence/emotion and vice-versa. Solitary items need further inspection, so take your time and look for missing beliefs or emotions. Practice several times with a pen and paper or a note-taking smartphone app. Use past situations for practice until you know what to do when you get hit with adversity.

Avoiding Unhelpful Thinking Patterns

There are several unhelpful thinking patterns that lower our mental and emotional resilience. The late psychiatrist Aaron Beck devised a list of seven unhelpful thinking patterns that increased the probability of developing depression in patients. They are also known as cognitive distortions. Over time, other psychologists, psychiatrists, and researchers uncovered many other cognitive distortions.

The original list consists of:

- personalization,
- overgeneralization,
- arbitrary inference (aka jumping to conclusions),
- minimization,

- magnification,
- selective abstraction (or mental filter),
- absolutistic dichotomous thinking (aka all-or-nothing thinking).

Examples of other cognitive distortions that you might be familiar with are perfectionism, obsessive-compulsive disorder, panic disorder, and phobias. However, we won't discuss them here.

1. Personalization

This cognitive distortion involves blaming yourself for anything and everything that happens around you. You may think that the source of a problem lies in something inappropriate you have said or done. Or maybe you believe you're just dumb or incompetent, and nothing you ever do works out. Instead of allowing you to assign responsibility to the correct party and find solutions to the problem, this unhelpful thinking pattern tends to make you a passive observer without any means to affect positive changes, both internally and externally.

There are two other facets of personalization: blaming others and victimization. In the former, instead of blaming yourself, you blame others for anything bad that happens around you. In the latter, if you believe others are out to get you but can't assume responsibility for your own failings and mistakes, then you're probably fond of victimization.

Examples of personalization include students who blame themselves for their poor performance in school, adults blaming themselves for their children's mistakes, and children blaming themselves for their parents' divorce. If a student blames his teacher for his poor performance, he is putting the responsibility on others. Additionally, that same student may believe his teacher hates his guts and wants nothing but to see him fail, indicating an unhealthy victim mentality.

If you suspect a tendency to personalize, blame others, or call yourself a victim in every situation, ask yourself if your emotions, behaviors, and feelings are rational and healthy. Are you zealously trying to protect your self-esteem? Ask friends and family for input, although they may not cooperate or be completely honest with you.

2. Overgeneralization

If you tend to be biased, prejudiced, or like to apply stereotypes to other groups, then you are a victim of overgeneralization. It's characterized by taking one idea or piece of information from one event and applying it to all other similar events. After overgeneralization, you tend to hold those ideas as immutable truths. It's very common for some people to jam personalization, victim mentality, or blame into their overgeneralizations.

A simple strategy to identify whether you or others are overgeneralizing or not is to look for words such as *always*, *never*, *everything*, *nothing*, *everybody*, or *nobody* in your or someone else's statements. Question whether your assessments are realistic and accurate or just overgeneralizations. If you have identified an offending unrealistic assessment, think of ways to improve the accuracy of the statement, perhaps by changing "always" to "often."

Examples of overgeneralization include:

- Doing poorly at a new activity, giving up, and never trying it again because you're "clearly wasting your time and you'll never improve."
- Giving up trying to find a romantic partner because your last date, despite having fun and laughing, stopped answering your texts the following day.
- Stopping at a couple of consecutive red lights while driving for your morning commute and thinking that you always get red lights in the morning.

- A team member forgets to attach some spreadsheets to their email once in a while and complains to others that he always does that.
- Your extended family forgot to call Grandma on her birthday; now you think nobody cares about her anymore.
- Since your favorite presidential candidate didn't win this year's election, you consider the whole electoral system a sham.

3. Arbitrary Inference

Arbitrary inference, also known as jumping to conclusions, is the process of "forming an interpretation of a situation, event, or experience when there is no factual evidence to support the conclusion or when the conclusion is contrary to the evidence."[6] It's sort of a shortcut your brain takes (just like overgeneralization) to make sense of the world around us without spending too many cognitive resources. In other words, we do it unwittingly because we are lazy, wish to save time, wish to ignore evidence to save face, or simply because we have no interest in the subject.

The process of jumping to conclusions is usually influenced by your biases, prejudices, personal experiences, the feelings you display at the moment, news you have read online, or any other sources you can think of. It can affect your relationships, your jobs, the way you handle difficulties, your self-esteem, and even your health. It can be especially disastrous for those suffering from anxiety and depression, but make no mistake: even healthy people are prone to making hasty judgments. People who jump to conclusions often have problems with anger management[7], perfectionism,[8] addictions,[9] and suicidal thoughts/behavior,[10] besides the aforementioned anxiety[11] and depression.[12]

Arbitrary inference is often divided into two subcategories: mind reading and fortune telling. When you believe you know what people are thinking when you believe they're judging you, have negative opinions of you, or want to hurt you without any evidence to back that up, you're engaging in arbitrary inference. The same goes for thinking that you know what will happen as if you were able to see future events in your personal crystal ball, and that often involves painful, embarrassing, or catastrophic consequences for you and your loved ones. Both mind reading and fortune telling are especially bad for performance and motivation.

Common examples of jumping to conclusion-bias are:

- Imagining that your significant other/children/friends have died in an accident when they haven't contacted you when they said they would.
- Believing that a bear is about to attack you when you hear a noise while camping in a forest at night.
- Predicting that your date tonight with someone you met online is going to go horribly wrong, and you'll stay single forever.
- Reading your boss's mind while discussing a pay raise ("he thinks I don't deserve a raise yet").

The way to fight arbitrary inference is to tell yourself that just because you're having a thought (whether it's jumping to a conclusion or not), it doesn't mean it's true. Another way is to see a thought as just that, nothing more, nothing less. If you can label it, even better: "This thought feels like I'm jumping to conclusions; what evidence do I have that makes this thought true?" (This technique is useful for all cognitive distortions, not just arbitrary inference).

Also, I'd like to add that not all arbitrary inference situations are negative. Sometimes, it's better to act first and think about it later if doing so will help you with your goals of survival and happiness. If you feel fear or a strange gut feeling, then it's better to be safe than sorry, wouldn't you agree?

4 & 5. Minimization and Magnification

Minimization and magnification are two polar cognitive distortions. Strangely enough, they can occur simultaneously.

- **Minimization**: the act of underestimating positive aspects of the self, another person, or a certain event.
- **Magnification**: also called catastrophizing, is the opposite. It involves the exaggeration of negative aspects of the self, someone else, or an event.

If you often make a mountain out of a molehill, tend to overthink possible threats or imagine worst-case scenarios, then you're probably engaging in magnification. Conversely, if you tend to undervalue your positive traits or the positive impact things have on your life, then you're engaging in minimization. David Burns, a best-selling psychiatrist who popularized Ellis' and Beck's cognitive behavioral therapy in the 1980s, explains that "It's like looking at things through a set of binoculars. From one end, your problems seem much bigger and more terrifying. But if you look through the opposite end, your positive qualities look small and insignificant."[13]

Some people also use minimization and magnification with risks without even realizing it. Telling yourself that "this lump on my left breast is probably nothing; I'll get it checked on my physical next year" is not only minimization of a potentially deadly form of cancer but also irresponsible (primarily to yourself, but also to your loved ones). Alternatively, smoking/injecting meth every day and saying, "It helps me stay alert. Otherwise, I wouldn't be able to do my job." is a common way of justifying addictions or certain antisocial behaviors and magnifying the supposed positive aspects.

Examples of minimization and magnification are:

- Believing that, because of your ethnicity (or socioeconomic background, or your astrological sign, or religion, or any other ridiculous claim), you're less likely to contract a venereal disease, so you rarely use protection when engaging in sexual acts.

- Noticing a small spot on your skin and immediately thinking it's skin cancer.
- Considering yourself the worst at your job/craft/specialty, although people often make positive remarks about your abilities.
- Getting into an argument with a family member, friend, or romantic partner, then believing the relationship is ruined.

If you have issues with magnification, ask yourself whether the situation or adversity you're experiencing is as catastrophic as it seems. When you realize you're engaging in minimization, consider that the things you do right are not always the product of luck but, in many cases, the result of your skills and sound judgment. Recognize that you have good qualities, not only negative ones.

6. Selective Abstraction

Selective abstraction happens when a person focuses only on one or more negative aspects of an experience to the detriment of all other aspects, including the positive ones. This unhelpful thinking pattern makes the person see the whole experience through the lens of that one negative aspect. One detail becomes the focus of the event, while all the other information is filtered out. We also call this mental filter or tunnel vision.

Here's what Aaron Beck had to say about this cognitive distortion:

> First, I discovered there were automatic thoughts... As I collected more material, I found that these patients were misinterpreting what I

> had to tell them quite a bit. Eventually, I noted that the misinterpretations fell into [unintelligible] categories. One was called selective abstraction—one I gave that name to—where they would take one little element and then see everything through just that one little element. One little mistake would seem to them to represent everything.[14]

This unhelpful thinking pattern may affect how individuals remember things and situations from their past, as they'll focus on the negative aspects of past experiences.

An interesting point of view provided by David Burns is that there are two types of mental filtering: a negative and a positive one. **Negative mental filtering**, he argues, is common in people who engage in rumination and self-criticism. **Positive mental filtering** involves focusing only on the positive aspects of any given event to the detriment of all negative ones, often used by people to explain their addictions—in a fashion similar to the minimization of risks.[15]

Some examples of **selective abstraction**:

- Take a test or examination and focus on the one or two mistakes you made despite your high score.
- Playing your musical instrument at a performance and believing nobody enjoyed it because some people didn't pay attention or clapped at the end of each song.
- Being in charge of the barbecue grill at a backyard party, burning a couple of hamburger patties, and vowing never to get near a grill again.
- Engaging in destructive behavior, such as abusing illicit drugs, alcohol, or tobacco, and focusing on the good feelings they provide while ignoring the potential negative consequences.

- Believing that your presentation was a failure because a couple of attendees were distracted or the feedback forms had a couple of negative comments.
- Despite having fun on a date with an attractive member of the opposite sex (or the same gender, depending on your orientation), you focused on the way the person mispronounced a word or the single mole on their neck, which turned you off completely.

These are just a few examples. I'm certain you can recognize this unhelpful thinking pattern either in yourself or in friends and family members. Questioning if you're ignoring certain aspects of a situation or how different you would see a situation if you turned the mental filter off are good ways to counter selective abstraction. REBT and CBT have similar methods to help you with this if you're interested in talking to a mental health professional.

7. Dichotomous Thinking

Dichotomous thinking is also known as all-or-nothing thinking, black and white thinking, or absolutist thinking. You can guess what this thinking style is about: a binary system of beliefs that leaves no space for any shade of gray. People who think in absolutes tend to behave in extreme ways as well. Thinking in this binary manner often leads to disillusionment and depression as reality is usually very different from what a black-and-white point of view to events in life offers.

Telltale signs that you're engaging in **dichotomous thinking** is to look for words that represent absolutes, such as *always*, *never*, *everybody*, *nobody*, *good*, *bad*, *best*, and *worst*.

Here are some examples:

- Loving or hating a new series on TV.
- Believing your house is absolutely filthy or spotless.

- Feeling completely depressed or euphoric about events in life.
- Lack of moderation in certain behaviors, such as binge drinking or complete abstinence.
- Perfectionism or complete negligence for responsibilities or tasks.
- Subscribing to the belief that people are always good or downright evil.

This kind of thinking style may lead to other problems, such as anorexia, obesity, depression, anxiety, borderline personality disorder, perfectionism, and suicide ideation. A way of dealing with **dichotomous thinking** is to look for blind spots in your thoughts about adversities. The question is whether there are other points of view or different explanations for what you're feeling and thinking. Learn to accept that life is full of ambiguity and fight your urge to label others' actions and motivations into neat descriptions. Being flexible rather than having rigid views and beliefs about the world is a better way of finding solutions to problems that life presents to you.

These are the main unhelpful thinking patterns. As mentioned before, there are many more. With some introspection, they are relatively easy to recognize in our own behaviors and thoughts. The following section is about **iceberg beliefs**, aka hidden beliefs, and they require a more proactive approach to identify.

Iceberg Beliefs

Most people react relatively predictably when a problem comes knocking at their door. In the previous section, I presented a table with a set of five belief-consequence pairs that psychologists identified as universal. Now, picture a situation when your feelings didn't match the circumstances of the adversity. Feelings that made you confused as they were not the ones that you were used to having in similar situations, for example, sadness or anxiety when anger would have been expected. Perhaps the intensity of the feeling was off, such as depression rather than a healthy level of sadness, fury instead of annoyance, or debilitating guilt when mild guilt would have been more appropriate.

When you experience these puzzling situations, the most likely answer lies in what professionals call "**iceberg beliefs**." They're "a deeply held belief about how the world ought to operate and how you feel you ought to operate within that world"[16]. And, as the name implies, they're in large part hidden, and we're most likely not even aware they're there.

Need some examples? Here you are:

- Everything I do in life must be perfect.
- Everyone must respect me and be fair to me.
- Life must be easy for me.
- People should always agree with my ideas.
- When I help others, they must show their gratefulness.
- Crying is for women and children only and should be done privately.
- The poor and homeless should stop being lazy and get a job.
- People shouldn't start things if they can't finish them.
- Men should be able to control their emotions at all times.
- People should be self-sufficient in all aspects of life.

The first three examples are mentioned when we discuss Albert Ellis's three main *musts* that lead to a disturbed emotional state in Chapter 1. But that doesn't mean people are fully aware of them. The other items you might have seen in friends, coworkers, or family members. I believe it's somewhat easy to recognize the above examples in others, but it's a different story when looking inside ourselves. When you become more aware of your own **iceberg beliefs**, you start to understand why you behaved, thought, and felt the way you did during confrontations with people you know and love. You will also come to see what your real core values and motivations are. Understanding the core values and motivations of the most important people in your life is a nice bonus, wouldn't you agree?

There are three categories of **iceberg beliefs**: control, achievement, and acceptance. Let's quickly go over them:

- **Control**: As the name suggests, it applies to people who wish to be in control at all times. The mere thought of being unable to control an adversity's outcome terrifies them. Not being in charge of events is unthinkable. If they can't have control, then that means they failed and thus are unlovable, or so is the reasoning that goes through their minds. On the other hand, when they do have control, they fulfill a deep-seated need. They are the quintessential control freak. Examples of control-based **iceberg beliefs**: "My success depends solely on my efforts," "Failure is not an option," and "Why can't people see that my ideas will lead us to success?" "I had better take care of this myself," "People who make mistakes are just lazy and/or stupid," "Children shouldn't be so loud when playing in the neighborhood," "Women shouldn't wear plaid miniskirts/vertical stripes/sweatpants."
- **Achievement**: The need to be successful at everything is another big **iceberg belief**. People who measure themselves in terms of their achievements believe success to be the most important thing in their lives. Two cognitive distortions, perfectionism and selective abstraction, tend to go hand in hand with this **iceberg belief**. Sometimes, the lines between control-based beliefs and achievement-based beliefs get blurred. Talk about a recipe for disaster: They will set high standards that are often impossible to achieve not only for

themselves but for others under their care. Don't even get me started on their extreme focus on mistakes and perceived imperfections. The following phrases will sound familiar to those achievement-oriented folks: "People should always display effort, initiative, and persistence to achieve their goals," "Giving up is for losers," and "Failure is for the weak."

- **Acceptance**: The ultimate goal here is to be loved and accepted. Being praised by others feels great, and it's sometimes perceived as an emotional high akin to those provided by recreational drugs. I mean, who doesn't like to be praised by those around us, especially the ones we respect the most? Do you know what those among us who have acceptance-based **iceberg beliefs** don't like? Conflicts and being slighted. The consequence of these two undesirables is often overreaction. Past experiences may lead to arbitrary inference in the form of fortune-telling and mind-reading. Here are common thought patterns: "I should be praised for my skills/performance/personality," "People should immediately like me when meeting me. Otherwise, it means something is wrong with me," "I need people to always have a positive opinion of me," "I must be liked by everyone, no exceptions allowed," and "I have to make others happy at all costs."

These are the main categories. What do you think is your main modus operandi when things go south? Stop and think about past experiences. Do you tend to try to control others? Do you crave acceptance and the need to be respected by everyone around you? Or do you prioritize your job above all else at the expense of your relationships and health? Be aware that it's completely possible to have a mix of the control, achievement, and acceptance categories.

There are a few ways **iceberg beliefs** hurt us. The first is a disconnect between our feelings and how we react to adversities, such as embarrassment instead of anger or anxiety instead of depression. This disconnect usually happens when we least expect it. It can lead to behaviors that don't correspond to the seriousness of the situation, sometimes leading to violence.

Here's a personal example of a disconnect of emotions and reactions: I was living by myself in an apartment after graduating from university and was in a relationship with a past girlfriend. We had been dating for three years at one point, so we had decided it was time for her to move in. A couple of days after we brought her stuff in, I opened the medicine cabinet in the bathroom and noticed the toothpaste tube was bent out of shape, like someone had squeezed it right in the middle. Oh, the horror! It made my blood boil. I said nothing because I figured it wasn't a big deal. I did sulk for a few minutes, though. When it kept happening, I always felt frustrated and angry, but I didn't know exactly why such a frivolous matter would create such a disproportionate reaction. Yes, talk about a waste of time getting angry at a stupid toothpaste tube! The **iceberg belief** that I had at that point in life was that everything I possessed had to be in good condition so friends and family would admire my tidiness and praise me (clearly an acceptance-based hidden belief). Since my girlfriend had no idea I had such a belief, she kept using the tube the way she had always done. The anger I felt was based on the idea that she was violating my rights, but the intensity of said anger was clearly excessive compared to the degree of the "crime."

The second way **iceberg beliefs** hurt us is that when two or more beliefs are triggered simultaneously, making decisions becomes difficult. Let's say John got offered an overseas position with not only better pay but also the opportunity to learn new skills that may lead to a C-level position in the future. There are a couple of problems, though: his wife just got pregnant with their second child, and the position is on the other side of the world, and he can't take his family with him as the assignment will last only a year. John knows his desire for achievement and acceptance has driven him throughout his career. However, he feels guilty for not being able to spend more time with his family due to the long hours required by his stressful job. His father neglected his family and was always absent, leading John to vow never to put his kids through the same disappointments. His mother manipulated him emotionally to satisfy her need for companionship and withdrew her affection whenever John displayed signs of independence. John's **iceberg beliefs** are, thus, a tough trio to deal with: A deep desire to provide for his family and be there for them, a need to be successful, and the necessity to be accepted by those around him. Needless to say, anyone in John's shoes would have a hard time deciding: Should he stay and spend more quality time with his family, or should he go and fulfill his career objectives?

The third way **iceberg beliefs** hurt us is the inability to experience a healthy range of emotions, such as happiness, anger, guilt, sadness, joy, and other feelings, at the right time, during the right circumstances, and in the right intensity. Hidden beliefs lock us in a loop of the same unhealthy negative feelings, disrupting our life goals and happiness. You've probably met one of those types who get furious at the slightest offense. Maybe you operate in that mode for the majority of your waking hours. The cause of that anger has an infinite combination of possibilities, one being acceptance or lack thereof. I had a neighbor back in Brazil when I was a kid who I believe was a victim of this **iceberg belief**. Let's call him Roberto. Roberto was older and bigger than me and most kids in the neighborhood. He only ever hung out with kids younger than himself. He often got angry at the stupidest things and would rant until we finally found something fun to do. Strangely enough, he was not a bully, at least not to people: He confessed, with a smile on his face, to torturing stray kittens with his cigarettes, which deeply disturbed me. Before I had decided that I wanted nothing to do with him because of that statement, me and the other kids would sometimes play video games or soccer at his house. On several occasions, we got a glimpse of the dynamics between him and his parents, which made me realize decades later why he behaved the way he did. His parents were always angry, shouting, and making snide, demeaning comments. I won't pretend to know what was going on in his mind, but I believe getting angry all the time was the only way he knew how to deal with difficulties. Despite being short-tempered, we, the younger kids, accepted him the way he was. He probably wasn't accepted by his peers or parents. I think hanging out with a younger crowd and torturing defenseless animals were outlets for his frustrations.

All right, so how do you go about detecting those pesky hidden beliefs? The three issues we discussed above are the things to look for, first and foremost. Here they are again:

- Look for disparities between your **beliefs** and the **consequences**. If you feel sad rather than angry, that's a sign **iceberg beliefs** have been triggered.
- See if you're having difficulty in making decisions.
- Check whether the intensity of your emotions, behaviors, and thoughts are proportionate to the **belief**.

So, when you go through the **ABC**, and the above signs pop up, look for **iceberg beliefs**. If nothing stands out, then you don't have to worry too much about having hidden beliefs. In fact, be wary of the possibility of looking for iceberg beliefs when none are being triggered during an adversity. If the common associations presented in the Consequences section are enough to explain the way you feel or behave when facing problems, then you don't need to bark up the wrong tree.

If you find signs that **iceberg beliefs** have been triggered, then you can ask the questions Karen Reivich and Andrew Shatté recommend in *The Resilience Factor: 7 Keys to Finding Your Inner Strengths and Overcoming Life's Hurdles* (2002)[17] to allow you to better understand what kind of belief is holding you back:

- What does that mean to me?
- What is the most upsetting part of that for me?
- What is the worst part of that for me?
- What does that say about me?

- What's so bad about that?

The authors came up with "what" questions rather than "why" questions because people tend to become defensive and feel intimidated when asked "why?" while "what" questions allow you to dig deep into what is blocking your path to happiness.

The questions above don't have to be used in the sequence presented. You don't even have to use all of them to dig deep. You have to basically go by feeling. Let me present an example:

I had a coworker from a previous job who moved on from education; let's call her Maria. Maria was an extremely attractive realtor in her late thirties, but she had difficulty maintaining romantic relationships. The usual pattern went like this: Maria met an interesting prospective partner, went on a few dates, started a serious relationship, and broke up after a few months. Sometimes, men would ghost her after a few dates or after a few weeks of exclusivity. Every time her partners broke up with her, she would feel less than human, something that men would use and discard once they felt she presented no more value to them. After breaking up, the cycle would repeat almost immediately, with only a few weeks between relationships. Every time that cycle repeated itself, she would feel shame and guilt, eat a bucket of ice cream while watching Netflix, then feel shame and guilt again, and finally hit the gym and run herself into the ground to compensate for the excess calories. Feeling shame or guilt doesn't seem to be a healthy response to her situation. If anything, people in her situation may feel anger for being disposed of so quickly without any effort from their partners to improve the relationship first. So, what belief could be at play when Maria feels guilt and shame rather than anger or sadness? Maria tells herself: "Men always break up with me once they get to know me. I feel ashamed and guilty because I should be able to keep a partner around for longer than a couple of months. That means there's something wrong with me!" Let's start uncovering **iceberg beliefs** by asking the "what" questions above.

Question: Men seem to break up with me right after getting to know me better. What does that say about me?

Answer: It means that I'm a bad person, that I'm not interesting, or maybe that I'm too busy or successful for my own good.

Question: What's the most upsetting part of that for me?

Answer: I think the worst part is being a bad person. I mean, some of my best friends are not super interesting people, but they're kind and supportive, and I love them. And being busy doesn't bother me. I guess I'm successful because I love my job, and to be successful in my line of business, you have to work hard!

Question: What does being bad mean to me?

Answer: I don't know, maybe I don't pay attention to my boyfriend's needs? Maybe I end up neglecting them by checking one last email or following up with a client one more time before the weekend starts. Sometimes, I feel exhausted and end up sleeping on the sofa without eating anything or even taking a shower. Sometimes, I only message them in the morning, and I know some people don't like waiting that long.

Question: All right, let's say you aren't paying attention to their needs. What's so bad about that?

Answer: Hmm...Well, I should be able to take care of them, you know, make them happy and content. If I'm too busy with my stuff, I won't have time to cook them a nice meal or go with them to the movie theater on a Saturday or Sunday. How will I be able to have a family in these conditions? I don't want to end up like my mom. She was always so busy with her career, and when Dad left, things only got worse. I guess he felt neglected. My sisters and I had to look out for ourselves most days of the week, you know.

And there you go. Maria's source of shame and guilt, rather than sadness when being dumped by her boyfriends, is that she was becoming her mom, who had problems being present not only for her husband but also for her daughters. She felt she was in prison, unable to escape her destiny, thus the feelings she had been experiencing. And now all she has to do is to just slow down, right? Not so fast. Maria, being so driven, was probably influenced by her mom's desire to be successful, triggering the achievement iceberg we discussed earlier.

Here's another example for you: My wife and I have had several conversations about how to raise a child in Japan. Obviously, we had disagreements, but we also agreed on some pretty important points. Problems would usually show up after I had had conversations with my sister—who has a daughter— and my brother—who has fifteen kids. At one point, I was really into the ketogenic diet and thought it was a good idea to limit the amount of carbohydrates and sugar our future child could consume. My wife also adopted the gluten-free diet for a period of half a year, even though she is not celiac. She told me that raising a child who couldn't eat carbs in Japan would burden her needlessly because everything has carbohydrates in Japan: school lunch, eating out, socializing with other children, you name it. Rice and noodles are staples of Japanese cuisine, as you know. That became a point of contention. When I learned that my sister, who introduced me to the keto diet, was not going to put my niece on a keto diet for basically the same reasons my wife had pointed out, I was happy to mention that to the wife. Instead of making fun of me or teasing me, she got upset, and we started a fight. The conversation went something like the following:

Me: My sister said she's not gonna limit the amount of sugar and carbs on her daughter's diet. I guess we should do the same when we have a child.

Her: What? That's what I said a couple of weeks ago! Why didn't you listen to me then?

Me: Why are you so angry?

Her: Of course I'm angry! What did you expect? You never listen to me!

Me: Never? That's not fair. There are plenty of situations where I listen to you. Besides, what's so bad about this? Can't I change my mind?

Her: You can, but this is not the first time something like this has happened. You listen to your sister but never listen to me when it comes to child-rearing.

Me: (not wanting to admit the truth) No way. Even if that were true, what does that mean to you?

Her: Are you deaf? I told you: it means you don't listen to me!

Me: What's the most upsetting thing about that for you?

Her: It feels like you don't care about my opinions. I say something, and it's in one ear and out the other with you.

Me: And what's the worst part of that?

Her: The worst part is that it feels like you don't pay attention to what I say. When that happens, I always think you don't love me. Simple as that.

We can say with confidence that this was an aha moment. The fight uncovered a hidden belief, that of acceptance. I later had to admit that my wife was right not only about the keto diet and children—it's not recommended unless the child suffers from severe epilepsy—but also that I was indeed taking my sister's opinion to the detriment of my wife's.

Sometimes, the questioning for uncovering **iceberg beliefs** is very straightforward; sometimes, you will ask questions that lead nowhere. Other times, the questions you ask will only help you to dig your heels in and justify your behavior and beliefs. That's normal. If you focus on "what" questions and practice a lot, you'll start getting a feeling for when you're moving forward or making no progress. You'll gradually become better at discovering your **iceberg beliefs**. A dead giveaway of finding them is when you think you have come to a stunning discovery, an "aha!" or "bingo!" moment. Another sign that you've made good progress is when you realize why some decisions seemed so difficult, when the feelings no longer feel excessive, or when they start to make sense.

After you have identified some of your **iceberg beliefs**, you need to ask yourself three important questions so you can evaluate their cost-benefit ratio. Here they are:

- What is the price I pay for this belief? In other words, what is its cost in my life?
- What do I get for this belief? In other words, how does it help me?
- How can I change this belief in order to increase the benefits and decrease the costs?

You may discover that some hidden **iceberg beliefs** are actually beneficial for some parts of your life. Be careful, however, in assuming that those beneficial beliefs are not holding you back in other areas of your life. Can you say with one hundred percent certainty that your need for control is acceptable or appreciated by all other people you could interact with in your life outside of your job? Or is your need for organization and cleanliness appropriate in all contexts? Hopefully, by asking yourself the three questions above and writing them down in a notebook or app, you can see clearly how these beliefs affect you.

Key Takeaways

- The **ABC model** helps you see how thoughts are the real source of negative feelings and behaviors that may not help you with your life goals. Therefore, adversity is not the source of misery per se; it is the way you interpret those events.
- There are five universal **Belief-Consequence** pairs that help predict how people may react when facing adversities: future threats lead to anxiety, comparison to others in a negative way leads to embarrassment,

infringements on your rights lead to anger, grief and loss lead to sadness, and infringements on others' rights lead to guilt.

- The correct order of the ABC method is to start with **Adversities**, compile the **Consequences**, and then figure out the **Beliefs**.
- Psychologists and other mental health professionals identified and researched several unhelpful thinking patterns, such as personalization, overgeneralization, jumping to conclusions, minimization, magnification, mental filter, and all-or-nothing thinking. They often influence our thoughts, feelings, and behaviors.
- **Iceberg beliefs** are hidden beliefs about how the world should be and how you should act in said world. Once uncovered, they help you understand why you experience feelings that don't match the situation, why the intensity of some feelings isn't appropriate for the adversity, or why you can't make certain important decisions.
- Karen Reivich and Andrew Shatté distilled a long list of **iceberg beliefs** into three main categories: **control**, **achievement**, and **acceptance**.
- To find your hidden beliefs, ask *what* questions rather than *why* questions.

All right. You have learned more about the **ABC model**, and how it can help you when you are faced with life's difficult problems. We're going to go into more details on how to make changes so you're better equipped to handle those problems.

---

1. Ellis, Albert. *Reason and Emotion in Psychotherapy*. (New York: Lyle Stuart, 1962).

2. Reivich, Karen, and Andrew Shatté. *The Resilience Factor: 7 Keys to Finding Your Inner Strength and Overcoming Life's Hurdles*. (New York: Broadway Books, 2002).

3. Epictetus. *The Enchiridion*. Translated by Elizabeth Carter. (London: George Bell and Sons, 1910).

4. Pittman, Catherine M., and Elizabeth M. Karle. *Rewire Your Anxious Brain: How to Use the Neuroscience of Fear to End Anxiety, Panic, and Worry*. (Oakland, CA: New Harbinger Publications, 2015).

5. Whitbourne, Susan K. "Guide to Guilt." *Psychology Today*, August 11, 2012.

6. Aaron T. Beck. *"Thinking and Depression: I. Idiosyncratic Content and Cognitive Distortions." Archives of General Psychiatry*. 1963, 9(4), 324–333.

7. Eckhardt, Christopher, and Howard Kassinove. *"Articulated Cognitive Distortions and Cognitive Deficiencies in Maritally Violent Men." Journal of Cognitive Psychotherapy, 1998, 12(3), 231–250.*

8. Davis, Melissa, and Nicole Wosinski. 2011. "Cognitive Errors as Predictors of Adaptive and Maladaptive Perfectionism in Children." *Journal of Rational-emotive & Cognitive-behavior Therapy*. 30. 1-13. 10.1007/s10942-011-0129-1.

9. Burns, David D. *Feeling Great: The Revolutionary New Treatment for Depression and Anxiety*. PESI Publishing. 2020.

10. Jager-Hyman, Shari, et al. "Cognitive Distortions and Suicide Attempts." *Cognit Ther Res.* Aug 1;38(4):369-374. doi: 10.1007/s10608-014-9613-0.

11. Blake, Emily, Keith S Dobson, Amanda R Sheptycki, and Martin Drapeau. 2016. "The Relationship Between Depression Severity and Cognitive Errors." *American Journal of Psychotherapy*, 70, 203-221. DOI: 10.1176/appi.psychotherapy.2016.70.2.203.

12. Blackburn, I. M., and K. M. Eunson. *Cognitive Therapy in Action*. (London: Sage, 1989).

13. Burns, David D. 2020. *Feeling Great: The Revolutionary New Treatment for Depression and Anxiety*. PESI Publishing.

14. Judith S. Beck, "Annual Reviews Conversations Presents: A Conversation with Aaron T. Beck," *Annual Reviews* (2012), https://www.annualreviews.org/userimages/ContentEditor/1351004835908/AaronTBeckTranscript.pdf

15. Burns, David D. 2020. *Feeling Great: The Revolutionary New Treatment for Depression and Anxiety*. PESI Publishing.

16. Reivich, Karen, and Andrew Shatté. *The Resilience Factor: 7 Keys to Finding Your Inner Strengths and Overcoming Life's Hurdles* (New York: Broadway Books, 2002).

17. Karen Reivich and Andrew Shatté, *The Resilience Factor: 7 Keys to Finding Your Inner Strengths and Overcoming Life's Hurdles* (New York: Broadway Books, 2002).

Chapter Three

Time to Change

> When we are no longer able to change a situation,
> we are challenged to change ourselves.
>
> Viktor Frankl, psychiatrist and psychotherapist

You now have some insight into what pushes your buttons. It's time to start thinking about how to make changes. You do that by becoming a scientist. No, I'm not going to ask you to enroll in a university course, start writing a thesis for a master's in electrical engineering or defend a dissertation on cosmology. It's much simpler than you think. We become scientists by following the scientific method, or better yet, an adapted version psychologists use.

So what is that? The scientific method consists of a few steps to develop theories of why you are behaving, feeling, and thinking the way you are when faced with adversities. Mind you, the scientific method is not perfect, nor is it infallible. Sometimes, the results will be incomplete. But that's okay since it allows us to try again and improve our knowledge little bit by little bit, allowing us a high degree of flexibility. And here is the heart of the method: we aren't simply rationalizing events and arriving at ideas and writing them in stone; we are constantly revising them and changing the underlying theories whenever new information comes along. Albert Ellis posits that, by using this method, we can see how irrational our beliefs, thoughts, and behaviors are and arrive at better alternatives.

There are two things to keep in mind here. The first is that we're not dealing with facts. When we talk about our feelings and thoughts, they can rarely, if ever, be considered facts. The same can be said about the theories we develop when following the scientific method: they're not facts, just hypotheses. The second is that nobody can apply scientific methods to dispute their irrational beliefs in a perfect manner. That means you won't be able to stop irrational beliefs from popping up in your mind, nor will you be able to always, 100% root them out and lead a perfect life without irrational beliefs. Whoever promises you that is probably a cult leader looking for new members to indoctrinate.

What follows are the basic steps of the scientific method proposed by Albert Ellis to challenge our beliefs:

1. **Observe**. Is the belief a fact? Is it realistic? It's in our best interest to accept things that are happening as reality, although we may not like them and try to change them. Constant observation and checking whether they're still true or have changed is the first step.

2. **Hypothesize**. Is the belief logical? Are there any contradictions? The second step is to state the hypotheses, the theories, and the scientific laws concerning the event logically and consistently, avoiding contradictions and unrealistic "facts." It's absolutely okay—expected even—to change the hypotheses once you learn they're not supported anymore by logic or facts.

3. **Be skeptical**. Is this a flexible belief? Is this belief true under all circumstances? Will it stay true until the end of times? The scientific method requires flexibility in its structure to stand the test of time. Science doesn't give too much weight to ideas claimed to be true under

all conditions until the end of times. This leads us back to the previous point: It revises previously set theories according to new information.

4. **Test it.** Can you refute this belief? Can you show this belief as false, i.e., can it be falsified? How can you and others challenge this belief? Again, there are limitations to what science can prove or disprove. For one, science cannot make affirmations about events or objects that cannot be observed, tested, and revised. That includes beliefs, spirits, supernatural beings, etc. If it can't be refuted, then it's not included in science.

5. **Question the merit.** Do you think the consequences of this belief are a result of good or bad karma? Can you say that the universe owes you anything or punishes you because of your belief? Value judgments like good and bad or "deservingness" and "undeservingness" are outside of the scope of science. That means science doesn't see the universe rewarding people because they behave in a good way or damning them for their bad deeds as possible. Groups of people, on the other hand, consider behaviors as good or bad and tend to reward individuals who display "good" behavior or punish individuals who display "bad" behavior.

6. **Keep your goals and standards in mind.** Does this belief prove I will behave in the right way to achieve my goals? Does this belief establish that I'll have a good life and achieve happiness? Science itself does not set any rules for human affairs and how people should conduct themselves in society. It does, however, study their living conditions, their behaviors, their personalities, and other factors once a large group of people has established goals and standards. Science can help people lead happy, healthy lives, but as always, it makes no guarantees.

Now that you've learned about some of the most important rules of the scientific method, you need to be able to apply them to your irrational beliefs and the emotional problems they cause. Let's have a few examples of this method in action. First, an irrational belief, then the method in action:

Irrational belief #1

People whom I admire and who are important to me must accept me and approve of everything I do. If they don't, then it means I'll be doomed to a life of pain and misery.

Scientific analysis:

1. **Is the belief a fact? Is it realistic?** No, this is not a fact, and it's not realistic. Where is it written that everyone around me must accept me and they have to approve of everything I do? Is there a law somewhere stating this? Has there been enough documented cases of people unconditionally accepting me and approving everything I do? No, no, and no. I may not like it when people don't approve or accept me, and an uncomfortable feeling may arise because of this, but that doesn't mean my life will end then and there when it happens.

2. **Is the belief logical? Are there any contradictions?** This belief clearly is not logical because I can't control what people do or think; that's just not how things work. This is not a mathematical equation where the end result of whatever I do and say equals approval and acceptance from everyone involved 100% of the time. It may not feel good when people I consider to be important don't accept me immediately, but that doesn't mean they will never ever accept things I do or say in the future. Alternatively, it could be something positive since I may learn more about them and find out that some of their values don't really match with mine or that they may abandon me in the most critical moments of my life.

3. **Is this a flexible belief? Is this belief absolutely true under all circumstances? Will it stay true until the**

end of times? The answer is a resounding *NO* since the belief states that people I care about and admire *must* accept me and approve of *everything* I do. This is obviously not true under all circumstances, and I cannot predict that it will remain true for the rest of my life. I don't think I could make this belief more rigid and inflexible if I tried.

4. **Can you refute this belief? How can you and others challenge this belief?** Yes, I can refute this belief. Again, it's easily demonstrable my inability to control others and demand that they accept me. People can and might disapprove of my actions and thoughts. That doesn't make me less of a person. Despite not being accepted or approved by most people, I can still work on my goals and happiness.

5. **Do you think the consequences of this belief are a result of good or bad karma? Can you say that the universe owes you anything or punishes you because of your belief?** No, I can't prove that because of the things I say and do, people will certainly approve of them. That's not how the world operates. No amount of belief in karma, God, spirits, or any other supernatural being will change this fact. It doesn't matter how eloquent I am, how much money or good looks I possess, or how nicely I ask; people won't simply accept or approve of me if they don't want to.

6. **Does this belief prove I will behave in the right way to achieve my goals? Does this belief establish that I'll have a good life and achieve happiness?** No, this belief won't help me achieve my goals, nor will it guarantee happiness. In fact, it might actually work against me. If people I care about don't accept me or approve of me, I might actually feel depressed and procrastinate or downright give up on working on my goals. And trying to make people accept me, but failing to do so may make me feel animosity toward them and myself.

Irrational belief #2

I must act competently because that's how I like to conduct my life.

Scientific analysis:

1. **Is the belief a fact? Is it realistic?** No, this is not a fact, and it's not realistic. I'm a human being, after all. I make mistakes just like everybody else. I do have the choice to act in such a way, but that doesn't mean I will be able to perform at the highest standard all the time. I may choose not to give my all in certain things in life, and that's totally acceptable.

2. **Is the belief logical? Are there any contradictions?** This belief clearly is not logical because I can't possibly do everything perfectly. No one in human history has proven that they can perform better than everyone else at everything. Being human contradicts the belief itself: how could I, a human being who is prone to make mistakes, expect to do everything competently?

3. **Is this a flexible belief? Is this belief absolutely true under all circumstances? Will it stay true until the end of times?** The answer is a resounding *NO* since the belief states that I *must* act competently. This implies that everything I do has to be perfect at all times, under all circumstances. No degree of flexibility is allowed. It's clearly a rigid belief.

4. **Can you refute this belief? How can you and others challenge this belief?** Yes, I can refute this belief. The reality is that I cannot do everything competently at all times; it's simply impossible. I could say that I do everything competently, but any sane, skeptical person will *NOT* take this statement at face value.

5. **Do you think the consequences of this belief are a result of good or bad karma? Can you say that the universe owes you anything or punishes you**

because of your belief? No, I can't prove that. Just because I *try* to do everything competently, the universe does not have to reward all my efforts with competence. How would I go about ensuring that, anyway? What I can do is expect to act competently in some situations, mostly due to my efforts, skills, and patience.

6. **Does this belief prove I will behave in the right way to achieve my goals? Does this belief establish that I'll have a good life and achieve happiness?** No, this belief won't help me achieve my goals, nor will it guarantee happiness. On the contrary, it might lead to undesirable results, such as suspicion, jealousy, and hate from others. They may even try to harm me. I may also feel dejected and disappointed in myself for failing to act competently at all times.

Irrational belief #3

I must always be treated fairly, respectfully, and carefully by others. If people don't treat me fairly, respectfully, and caringly, they are bad, evil, and miserable and must be punished and criticized.

Scientific analysis:

1. **Is the belief a fact? Is it realistic?** No, this is not a fact, and it's not realistic. Just because I want people to treat me in that manner, they don't have to. In fact, some people will downright treat me badly for the simple fact that they can. No matter how nice or respectful I treat some people, they won't match my level of courtesy. That doesn't make them evil. There are people that we consider bad who actually do act in neutral ways or even perform good deeds. Can I really say that everyone who treats me in a less-than-nice way deserves to be punished? Obviously not.

2. **Is the belief logical? Are there any contradictions?** This belief clearly is not logical because I cannot

state that every individual who treats me badly is consequently a horrible, vile person and deserves to be criticized and punished. Would you consider family members, friends, coworkers, and neighbors who have treated you badly in the past as totally wicked people?

3. **Is this a flexible belief? Is this belief absolutely true under all circumstances? Will it stay true until the end of times?** The answer is a resounding *NO* since the belief provides no wiggle room: everyone, no exceptions allowed, should treat me really well, forever and ever, until the day I die. The reality is that not everyone who treats me in an aggravating way is evil and thus deserves punishment.

4. **Can you refute this belief? How can you and others challenge this belief?** Yes, I can refute this belief. It's very easy to see the fallacy of such a belief: Just because some people treat me in an awful way, that doesn't mean they are rotten to the core, nor does it mean they have to be penalized. Unless I state that the people who treated me badly have not been punished yet, but they will certainly be, possibly in the afterlife, then yes, it can be refuted.

5. **Do you think the consequences of this belief are a result of good or bad karma? Can you say that the universe owes you anything or punishes you because of your belief?** No, I can't prove that. I can't say nor provide evidence that everyone who treats me badly is evil. The same goes for the idea that because they treated me badly, they were (or will be) punished for such transgression by an invisible, omniscient, and omnipotent force or entity. Can it really be said that other people's actions toward me are bad? Some people, upon seeing this, may have a different opinion; they may think it was actually something good or just neutral.

6. **Does this belief prove I will behave in the right way to achieve my goals? Does this belief establish**

that I'll have a good life and achieve happiness? No, this belief won't help me achieve my goals, nor will it guarantee happiness. If I hold this belief, I'm bound to experience disappointment, which will most likely lead to anger and other related emotions. I might not even be able to see why they treat me in such a manner. I might not be able to work with them on compromises. Or I might develop a victim complex. What's more, I'll waste time thinking about those who treated me unfairly and their perceived offenses or get into heated arguments with them. How does this help with my goals and happiness?

I hope these three examples helped you see what these beliefs really are: irrational, illogical, inflexible, and refutable. The scientific method allows people to fight their irrational beliefs, providing great help in difficult times. But do keep in mind that, just like science, it's not a panacea. It can't guarantee that every single adversity you face will dissolve like sugar in a glass of water.

ABCDE

You now know how to apply the scientific method to dispute your beliefs. Another technique you can use that builds on the scientific method is called the **ABCDE**, an extension of the original **ABC model**. While the latter allows you to become aware of what is going on at the moment of the adversity (or after), the former is another tool that allows you to affect real change. In his book *How to Stubbornly Refuse to Make Yourself Miserable About Anything-yes, Anything!*, Albert Ellis' **REBT** provides us with a list of fourteen insights. In my opinion, one of the most important ones is number five, which states, "Fully acknowledge that you upset yourself with irrational musts. Acknowledging that you have musts will not in itself make them disappear. Fight them in many ways that **REBT** provides, but above all actively challenge and dispute them"[1]

What do the letters **D** and **E** in this model mean?

- **D** stands for **Disputing**. You are basically questioning yourself in order to see how irrational your beliefs are and why they are affecting you.
- **E** stands for **Effective New Philosophy**. This will provide you with new rational beliefs and better life philosophies.

Some psychologists subscribe to the **ABCDEF** model, where the letter **F** stands for new **Feelings**. These new feelings provided by this model may lead to new, appropriate behaviors that align with your goals in life.

The **ABCDE** model doesn't implement all of the questions from the previous section. Instead, you have a dialogue with yourself—or rather, a monologue—and choose the most appropriate questions. There's no cheating yourself here. You have to honestly answer your own questions in a rational, logical way. It's worth reminding you that no technique used in this book, including the scientific method, will get rid of negative feelings for you. You can certainly try, but good luck with that. Feelings, positive and negative alike, are a natural brain process. You can and should learn to classify those feelings as either healthy or unhealthy. Which do you think is a healthy negative feeling: mildly bothered by adversity or incensed? Which is likely to help you achieve your goals or implement changes in life?

Let's get back to the subject of changing your irrational beliefs. The first step is to use the **ABC** for each objective or goal, like so:

Goal: "I want to find a girlfriend/boyfriend."

Adversity: "I go on dates with potential partners, but none go past the first or second dates."

Rational Belief: "Going on dates is fun, but I'd rather find a more stable relationship. Since I can't seem to get that, it's honestly very demotivating. How can I improve my chances of actually landing a boyfriend/girlfriend?"

Irrational Beliefs: "I must make a potential partner like me on the first date! If that doesn't happen, they'll never contact me again, and I'll never find the true love of my life. That's terrible; I just hate the thought of never finding anyone who will love me. If I don't find anyone soon, I'll live a dull, loveless life, and I'll die all alone."

Consequences: I feel sad, lonely, and ashamed. I stop trying to find potential partners.

We have now defined a goal and determined what the adversity is (the letter **A**), the rational and irrational beliefs (the letter **B**), and the consequences (the letter **C**). Remember that you should work on your **A**s first, then your **C**s, and finally your **B**s. It's time to start the second step: disputing the irrational beliefs in a logical, rational way, the scientific way. We will separate the irrational beliefs into chunks, dispute them one by one (the letter **D**), and then provide effective new philosophies (the letter **E**). Let's take a look at how you could do this:

Irrational Belief Part 1. "I must make a potential partner like me on the first date!"

Dispute: "Why *must* I make someone like me on the first date?"

Effective New Philosophy: "I don't have to make someone like me or fall in love with me on the first date. Of course, if someone I'm attracted to does fall in love with me, that would be cool. But if they don't, that's fine as well, as that would allow us to get to know each other better and decide if we are a good fit for each other. I wouldn't feel all right if I had to reject someone whom I don't feel attracted to personality-wise is clearly head over heels for me.

Irrational belief part 2: "If that doesn't happen, they'll never contact me again, and I'll never find the true love of my life."

Dispute: "Is there any evidence showing that this is the only outcome?"

Effective New Philosophy: "Although the majority of first dates never led to a second date in the past year, many people have indeed contacted me after the first date. I did experience fulfilling romantic relationships in the past, so there's no evidence that I'll never experience it again in the future."

Irrational belief part 3: "That's terrible; I just hate the thought of never finding anyone who will love me."

Dispute: "How is this terrible?"

Effective New Philosophy: "It's not terrible at all. It may not feel good, but it's a temporary situation. It doesn't mean I will forever be rejected. There are so many people in this world who are compatible with me; I just need to keep looking. Besides, getting rejected is a real possibility, as I can't force people to love me. I may have one or two traits that the potential partner doesn't like, so they decided to reject me. That's fine. I can't possibly love all potential love partners, either. Some of them surely have some negative aspects that I may consider a deal breaker in the future. Instead of being terrible, this situation is simply annoying. The thought of never finding anyone is just that, a thought. I can hate it or love it, and it bears no relation to reality."

Irrational belief part 4: "If I don't find anyone soon, I'll live a dull, loveless life, and I'll die all alone."

Dispute: "Why does it have to be soon? Do I know for certain how I will die? Where is it written that this is my fate?"

Effective New Philosophy: "My brain created these irrational ideas that I must find someone soon and that if I don't, I'll live a dull life and will die alone. I can be perfectly happy without a partner for life, as many people can attest. Life is not just a collection of romantic partners; it's much more. Friends, family, hobbies, new experiences, and work all contribute to a healthy life. If I really want a family and don't want to die alone, I can consider adoption. That won't guarantee that I will be able to choose how I die, though."

And there you have an example. Don't think that doing it once or twice will make you an expert. It won't. You do need to practice it many times until irrational beliefs (including cognitive distortions) no longer have a tight grip on you. When you feel confident in your capacity to question yourself honestly, you'll notice the consequences of your irrational beliefs also change. Your behavior, once plagued by self-doubt, procrastination, inaction, and negative self-talk, will change and align with your life goals and values. Instead of lamenting that you can't find a partner who will love you for the rest of your life, you can focus on other aspects of your life, create new goals, try different venues to meet potential partners (e.g., online dating apps/websites, speed dating events, hobbies, classes, bars), learn new things, help out at charity organizations, etc.

What follows is a list of common irrational beliefs compiled by Albert Ellis. See if any of these apply to past experiences. You might notice some overlap between this list and the three categories of **iceberg beliefs** created by Karen Reivich and Andrew Shatté: control, achievement, and acceptance. Here they are:

- **Awfulizing, horribleizing, and terribleizing**: close relatives of magnification and catastrophizing. This triad implies that adversities are more than bad, which leads to anxiety and depression. Reality is probably less horrible than it seems. Ask yourself: could things actually be worse than they are, or is this really the apex of how awful things could get? Here's a quick example of awfulizing: "Things in my house must be organized alphabetically; if they're not, it's horrible because it shows how much of a slob I am, and nobody likes a slob."
- **Perfectionism and grandiosity**: Perfectionism is a separate category of cognitive distortion with some overlapping with all-or-nothing thinking; grandiosity is associated with feelings of superiority, invulnerability, and uniqueness. A person with these irrational beliefs could think, "I must be perfect, and people must see how unique and special I am. Otherwise, I'm nothing. If

I can't be extraordinary, then I'm not worthy or good."

- **Worthlessness and self-hatred**: both involve low self-esteem and feelings of inferiority, inadequacy, and guilt. Both can lead to a lack of motivation, depression, hopelessness, and feelings of powerlessness. For instance, someone suffering from feelings of worthlessness and self-hatred might think, "Since I failed once again to try to give up meth, I'm doomed to repeat this cycle of trying to quit and always failing. This just proves how worthless and incompetent I am. I mean, how can someone be so bad at it? It just proves that I suck as a human being."

- **Self-damnation and undeservingness**: these tend to show up when we make mistakes. These mistakes tend to be interpreted in a harsher way than a mentally resilient person would. These irrational beliefs are closely associated with shame and guilt. After hurting a loved one, someone might think, "I deserve to burn in hell for hurting my mom like that. Who does such a thing? I must not hurt her again like that. If I do, then I don't deserve forgiveness, and I hope I get punished because that's what people who hurt their parents deserve."

- **Low frustration tolerance, a.k.a. "*I can't-stand-it-itis*"**: when we experience being overwhelmed by circumstances or being outside of our comfort zones, leading to a lack of desire to engage with challenges or new experiences. An example: "I hate flying. It boggles my mind to think about being stuck in a flying metal cage for ten hours. I shouldn't have to do it to attend a stupid training session across the world. Haven't they heard of online meetings or video conference software? I can't stand this stupidity. My manager should know that some people like me can't stand flying."

- **Belief in totality, allness, and neverness**: This is Ellis' version of the absolutistic dichotomous thinking, or all-or-nothing thinking. Here's an example: "Why did my girlfriend decide to adopt a dog? Can't she see how dangerous they are? I'll never be able to hang out with her at her place again. I shouldn't have to compete with a dog for her attention. This is ridiculous. She knows I don't like dogs. I'll never touch a dog again, no matter how much she pleads with me."

To make your life easier, here are common questions you can use to scientifically dispute your beliefs:

- Where is it written that my irrational belief is true? Can I say with 100% certainty that it exists in reality? Who, with absolute authority and knowledge, can testify to its authenticity?
- How can I support this belief and prove it's justified?
- Why doesn't this belief contradict reality? Why is it true?
- What facts support this belief?
- What kind of good and bad outcomes will I experience if I keep this belief?
- Can I stop believing this irrational belief?

Whenever you're afflicted by unhealthy feelings and their corresponding irrational beliefs, use the questions above to dispute them. Do it as many times as needed, and do it whenever you feel depressed, angry, and anxious or when you start hating or pitying yourself. Persevere, and you shall become victorious.

The Fast Skills

There are two skills you can use when you face a really tough situation and your emotions get out of whack: relaxing techniques and real-time resilience. They are quite useful if you don't have the time or inclination to use the ABCs or the scientific method.

These skills can be useful for three kinds of people:

- the type of person who loves to multitask and sleep four hours a night,
- the compulsive worrier with unending internal chatter,
- the aggressive and unreasonable who often loses control.

If you recognize yourself in any of the categories, then you know how easy it is to lose your focus, your serenity, or your head when someone or something pushes your buttons.

These three types of lifestyle may lead to excessive stress and sickness, strained family life or relationships, and wasted hours that could have been used productively toward your life goals. If you have problems sleeping or experience pains and aches here and there, then your stress might be out of control. Whether or not that is true for you, learning the following techniques may prove to be a great addition to your life.

Relaxing Techniques to Decrease Stress

It's impossible to avoid stress completely, and you probably wouldn't want to anyway since it can be a factor for positive change and motivation. Still, dealing with stress is an important aspect of being more resilient. And the way to manage stress is by learning how to relax. Being stressed out and relaxed at the same time is impossible. They're opposing states of the body. What follows are some simple relaxation techniques. Not all of them are going to work equally well for you. That's all right. Find the one that you feel is the most effective. You can try several techniques, one after the other as well.

Breathing

Have you noticed that your breathing gets shallower and faster when you get stressed out and anxious? If you pay enough attention, you'll also see that your chest is expanding and contracting. Your jaw muscles and your neck might feel tense. Now, go take a look at a baby sleeping in a crib. Notice how the baby breathes using her belly. And that's how we should breathe, at least in those stressful moments of everyday life. By using your belly and engaging your diaphragm, you slow down your body, allowing it to enter a relaxed state.

There are countless breathing techniques. Let's focus on **pranayama** breathing techniques. **Pranayama** is an ancient yoga practice, or component, that focuses on regulating the breath. It is often used together with yoga poses and meditation. The techniques presented in this book are based on pranayama, but for our purposes, they are used independently without the yoga poses or exercises.

According to science, some of the benefits of **pranayama** include lowered blood pressure[2], reduced reactivity of the amygdala and anxiety[3], improvements in aggression and negative emotional regulation[4], lung strengthening for asthma and other respiratory conditions[5], and reduced cravings in smokers[6].

Read below about the main techniques based on **pranayama**: the **4-7-8**, the **4-4-4-4**, and the **three-part breath breathing techniques**. After these techniques, we'll discuss **progressive muscle relaxation (PMR)**, **mindfulness**, and **guided imagery**.

4-7-8 Breathing

The **4-7-8 breathing pattern** or technique was created by Dr. Andrew Weil. He called it "a natural tranquilizer for the nervous system."[7] I've covered this technique in two previous books. That's how much I like it. I'm confident it will benefit my readers. Some people may feel a bit lightheaded when first trying the technique. Others feel nothing, even after trying it for a few days. Here are the basics:

1. Rest your tongue on the back of your top teeth. Breathe

out all the air in your lungs with your mouth open.

2. Close your mouth and inhale through your nose for a count of four.

3. Hold your breath and count to seven.

4. Breathe out for a count of eight. Make a "whoosh" sound as you do it.

5. Repeat the previous steps three more times.

The important thing to keep in mind is that when you exhale for a count of eight, it should feel slightly longer than when you're holding the air in. Go for a maximum of eight cycles if you feel that four cycles aren't enough. Practicing the **4-7-8** twice a day is a good way to create some muscle memory. That way you can use the technique effectively when the going gets tough.

When doing the **4-7-8 technique**, try as much as you can to engage your diaphragm both when you inhale and exhale. Put a hand on your belly and another on your chest. Practice diaphragm breathing and notice your belly going up and down (if you're lying down). I find lying down way easier to do the technique, but sometimes we don't have the luxury. So practice it on your bed in the beginning and then transition to standing practice.

4-4-4-4 Breathing

Now that you know a little about the **4-7-8 breathing technique**, let me introduce you to the **4-4-4-4 breathing technique**. I bet you already know what it's about. If you have no idea what I'm talking about here, it's another breathing technique similar to the **4-7-8** one, but with a different pattern.

Here's how you do it:

1. Exhale the air in your lungs completely.

2. Inhale through your nose for a count of four.

3. Hold your breath for a count of four.
4. Exhale while counting to four.
5. Hold that configuration and count to four with your lungs empty.
6. Restart the cycle. Repeat at least three more times.

I usually do the **4-4-4-4** breathing pattern right after the **4-7-8 breathing technique** while in bed before sleeping. I do eight cycles of each for a duration of about five or six minutes. I found this to be the optimal configuration for when I'm too tired to sleep or not tired enough. Your mileage may vary.

Three-Part Breath

The **three-part breath** is another great breathing practice for beginners. As the name implies, it's separated into three different parts. The process is as follows:

1. Lie or sit down in a comfortable position. Rest one hand on your chest and another on your belly.
2. Breathe naturally a few times, relaxing your muscles and noticing your thoughts coming and going. Exhale all the air in your lungs before starting.
3. Start the first part by inhaling and exhaling through your nose five times, filling only your belly in the process.
4. When you exhale, use your belly muscles to drive out all the air, imagining you're trying to touch your belly button to your spine.
5. Start the second part by filling your belly first and then your chest. Notice your rib cage expanding after your belly is "full."
6. When you breathe out, empty your chest first, then your belly. Repeat five times total.

7. The third part is the same as the second, but with a small difference: inhale, fill your belly, then your chest, and finally, take one last sip of air, filling the top part of your chest near the collar bones.

8. Continue for a total of five repetitions.

Things to keep in mind when practicing the three-part breath:

- You can make sure you're using only your belly by checking your hand going up and down on it. As you become more experienced, you won't even need to put your hands on your belly or chest.
- Try to maintain a slow and deliberate pacing of your breathing.
- Avoid inhaling too hard or straining too much. There should be a smooth flow to the practice. You shouldn't feel any pain.
- This type of pranayama is done with the eyes closed and sitting. However, you can leave your eyes open and lie down on the floor or bed until you get the hang of it.
- If you have asthma or another respiratory condition, take care not to overdo it. You should stop at any sign of dizziness.
- The process doesn't have to end after the fifth repetition. You can continue for another five repetitions or even more if you want.

Progressive Muscle Relaxation

Progressive muscle relaxation (PMR) was created by Dr. Edmund Jacobson and presented to Harvard University in 1908. It was later published and commonly recognized in 1938.[8] Dr. Jacobson found that excessive muscle tension and physical and mental disorders were connected. **PMR** is a great way to manage panic attacks and anxiety.

The process is quite simple, and anyone can learn it in a session or two. It has been studied by several universities, and there are few contraindications. It can improve your sleep quality[9], lower your blood pressure[10], lower the frequency of migraines[11], ease low back pain[12], and decrease anxiety, stress, and depression[13].

Here are the steps for the **PMR**:

1. Curl your toes up as tightly as you can. Hold for ten seconds. Relax. Lift your toes in the opposite direction for ten seconds. Relax for ten to twenty seconds.

2. Tighten your calves hard for ten seconds. Relax for ten to twenty seconds. Point your feet toward your knees, and hold for ten seconds. Relax for ten to twenty seconds.

3. Contract the muscles in your thighs as hard as you can for ten seconds. Relax for ten to twenty seconds. (If you're lying down, you can also lift your hips and your legs, keeping only the heels in contact with the floor for ten seconds. Relax for ten to twenty seconds.)

4. Work on the glutes for ten seconds. Relax for ten to twenty seconds.

5. Contract your belly for ten seconds. Relax for ten to twenty seconds.

6. Tighten the muscles in your chest as best you can for ten seconds. Relax for ten to twenty seconds.

7. Raise your shoulders to your ears. Keep that position for ten seconds. Relax for ten to twenty seconds.

8. Make fists with both hands, tightening the muscles in your fingers and forearms as much as you can. Hold for ten seconds. Relax for ten to twenty seconds.

9. Bend your arms and contract your upper arms for ten seconds. Relax for ten to twenty seconds.

10. Tense your neck by looking up and holding it for ten seconds. Repeat for all four directions. Relax for ten to twenty seconds when you finish.
11. Purse your lips together for ten seconds. Open your mouth wide for ten seconds. Relax for ten to twenty seconds.
12. Shut your eyes tightly for ten seconds. Relax for ten to twenty seconds.
13. Frown your forehead for ten seconds. Relax.

Some of those steps might prove too much for people with severe chronic conditions. If that's your situation, you can skip the contraction phase altogether and, instead, focus only on relaxing each muscle group.

You don't have to follow the sequence above to the letter. You can (and should) adapt it to your needs. However, try the sequence above in the first couple of weeks, perhaps doing it twice daily to get the hang of it. When you feel comfortable with the sequence, you can switch things up and work on the muscles that matter to you.

I personally skip the eyes, but I always add the upper and lower back, as well as the triceps (the muscles at the back of your upper arms). Also, if you wish to start slowly, for whatever reason, decrease the contraction phase to five seconds, then increase it when you're ready. Try different lengths for the contraction and relaxation phases to match your needs.

And how are you supposed to use the **PMR** in a stressful situation away from home? The best way to do it is to make an inventory of the biggest offenders. When you're stressed out, where do you feel tense? Is it your neck? Maybe your shoulders get more and more tense as the event progresses. Or is your lower back giving you trouble? Take notes of what you feel and in what parts of your body you feel it. Now that you know where the tension builds up, start your **PMR** routine by focusing on those muscles. Skip the ones that you feel have no stress or a low level of stress. Practice working on the offending muscles twice a day at home for at least two weeks.

Now, try using your new, shorter **PMR** routine while engaging in an activity. That will help you multitask. Try a few **PMR** sessions while watching TV at home, playing with the kids, and doing house chores. Move on to other venues, such as the supermarket, the bank, your office, during a meeting. The idea here is to gradually go from easiest to hardest.

*Just a quick heads-up about **PMR**: you may experience three different issues when first trying it out.*

The first is difficulty in relaxing. You may actually experience the opposite, as your muscles start to get tenser and tenser. This happens to people who experience high levels of anxiety and those who can't relinquish control. Some sexual assault victims may also have problems with **PMR**. If you somehow fit into these descriptions, you may find that your breathing becomes shallow and quick, and your heart rate may get elevated. Use the questions we discussed in the previous chapter to uncover any **iceberg beliefs** you may have. If no **iceberg beliefs** are present, use the **ABC** technique to put your unwillingness to relax into perspective.

The second issue related to PMR is that some people have problems isolating muscles. If you're physically inactive by choice, then maybe it's time to start an exercise program. Try calisthenics, weight lifting, Yoga, or pilates. They are great for your overall health and will teach you how to isolate muscles. I already hear some people complaining. Look, I get it. You hate exercising, or are too busy, or have arthritis. We all have problems, especially when we get older. But think about how your life could be improved with the right exercise program. Talk to your doctor. She can help you find the appropriate exercise for you and your condition. Or just go ahead and start PMR on your own. The process of learning to isolate the muscles will come naturally over time. You just need patience and perseverance. Besides, it's free and feels great, especially after a long day at work.

The last issue is falling asleep midway through PMR. This might not be a problem at all, depending on your situation. I myself use it as part of my bedtime routine when I can't fall asleep, usually after the **4-7-8** and the **4-4-4-4** breathing techniques. However, trying to relax in the morning, during work, or at other times throughout the day and immediately dozing off is clearly not a good idea. In that case, you might want to improve your sleep first. Consult a sleep clinic if your sleeping issues are too deep to treat on your own.

Mindfulness

Mindfulness is what scientists call meditation (for the purpose of this book, I will use the terms **mindfulness** and **meditation** as synonyms.) The objective of **mindfulness** is to improve one's awareness of not only one's environment but also what happens inside one's body and brain. Meditation provides several benefits, including lower blood pressure[14], positive changes to the immune system, loss of anxiety, as well as depression and stress[15], improved memory[16], and improved planning, self-control, and focus[17].

A crucial point of **mindfulness**, or any other type of meditation, is to try to avoid passing judgment. What does that mean? Simple: you don't evaluate any experience you have while meditating. Easier said than done, trust me. Thoughts about past experiences, predictions of what will happen in the near or distant future, emotions, outside stimuli like noises, light, vibrations, smells, or internal ones like pain, discomfort, and feelings are all examples that the meditator notices and lets go of. That is the essence of non-judgment.

To make things a wee bit easier on you, I advise using your breath as an anchor. What's an anchor? It's the "object" of your attention while meditating. Why do you need one? You use an anchor to stop paying attention to random experiences like that itchy patch of skin on your leg, the electricity bill due this Friday, or the poor, neglected dog barking non-stop next door. You see, when humans, since times immemorial, decided to sit down and meditate, they soon found that it was impossible to stop thoughts from being made in the brain. They devised a simple mechanism to help them get back to the task of meditating: paying attention to their breath. That way, whenever they lost concentration and realized they were distracted by mundane thoughts and feelings, they could go back to being present in the moment just by focusing on their own breath.

Now that we have the introduction out of the way, let's talk about how you do **mindfulness**:

1. Find the most comfortable position possible without falling asleep. Try sitting on a chair, on the floor, on the bed, or even standing if you wish. You can close your eyes or leave them open.

2. Focus on your breath. Inhale through your nose, and count one. Exhale through your mouth or nose, and count two. Repeat until you reach ten. Start over after that.

3. Your mind will drift to all manner of thoughts. That's to be expected. Just bring your focus back to your breathing and restart from one.

Here's another way of doing a breathing meditation:

1. After you find a comfortable sitting (or lying down) position, close your eyes.

2. Inhale through your nose and exhale through your mouth a few times. Then, let your breath return to its natural pattern.

3. Inhale, then count "one" as you exhale. You don't need to vocalize: do it silently.

4. Count "two" the next time you exhale. Do this all the way to "five."

5. Restart the cycle, counting every time you exhale.

If you're new to meditation, start small until you get used to the process. Start with a two-minute session in the morning (and another short one during the day if you have the time). Add two minutes to the morning session every week, all the way to thirteen minutes or more. Why thirteen? Because that's the amount of time researchers from New York University found to be beneficial for beginners. They found that eight weeks of short sessions were enough to improve memory and attention[18].

When you start the practice, always remember not to get upset or frustrated when you get distracted by random thoughts. Getting distracted is normal. You'll become better and slowly improve your focus power. Try not to rate the experience as good or bad. Don't get angry and tell yourself that you'll never learn how to do this damned thing. You just need patience. And above all else, consistency trumps quality. You stand to gain a lot more by doing a little **mindfulness** every day than doing long, forty-minute sessions once a week.

Guided Imagery

This calming technique involves creating relaxing, imaginary scenarios in your head. You can also imagine yourself performing at a high level in a sports competition, negotiations, presentations, or a test. Imagery works by "slowing down" the amygdala, two structures deep inside your brain responsible for survival and emotion processing, among other crucial functions. Benefits include improved sleep and decreased sense of pain, anxiety, and depression[19].

Examples of relaxing scenarios are deserted tropical beaches, beautiful prairies, quiet canyons, and cool forests. Some people experience greater levels of relaxation with imagery compared to PMR. Some others unfortunately can't imagine calming scenarios or relax at all.

The process for doing guided imagery or visualization is as follows:

1. Find a comfortable and quiet place to sit or lie down.

2. With your eyes closed, breathe in and out in a deliberate manner.

3. Imagine yourself in a location that brings you peace and comfort, like a beautiful beach.

4. Imagine all the details, such as the sounds, smells, and temperature on your skin.

5. Visualize yourself walking on a path through that location. What sounds can you hear? What do you feel on your skin or feet?

6. As you continue to breathe slowly and deeply, you feel your body relaxing more and more.

7. After fifteen minutes, slowly count backward from ten to zero. Slowly become aware of your environment. Open your eyes when you reach zero.

A few points about guided imagery:

- It's all right if you want to start small. A five-minute session in the first few days is completely fine.

- If you have difficulties creating a detailed image in your head, go ahead and download a smartphone app or play a YouTube video. Use your phone's *Do Not Disturb* mode while you're at it.

- Don't like what's available online? Are apps charging too much money or showing too many ads? No worries, create your own guided imagery. Write it down and read it during your next few sessions until you memorize it, or record it using your smartphone and play it whenever you want.

- Don't despair if you can't relax or create any detailed scenarios. That might mean your brain doesn't like to give up control—yet. Victims of sexual abuse may panic when listening to soft, relaxing voices. Or, if you have suffered from trauma, you may have problems focusing on the process. Keep at it, persevere, and your brain will slowly get used to it and finally start relaxing.

- A tip that may help you is not to worry whether the process is working or not. If you fall asleep, zone out, or think about other things (hopefully positive things), it will still be beneficial to you. Many people don't feel any change right away.
- As mentioned, you can use guided imagery in preparation for stressful situations such as interviews or discussions. Focus on the source of stress itself and imagine yourself handling the situation. Practice a few weeks in advance if at all possible.
- It may take several weeks before you feel the benefits in a perceptible way. If, after trying your best for a few weeks, you still feel uncomfortable or distressed, there is no shame in setting it aside for a couple of months or even in stopping guided imagery outright.

Focusing Techniques to Fight Unhelpful Thoughts

There are dozens of different types of cognitive distortions, also called unhelpful thinking patterns. I have already introduced the main ones, devised by Aaron Beck and David Burns, in Chapter 2. Other cognitive distortions, such as emotional reasoning (an emotional reaction "proves" that an event is true, despite evidence to the contrary), gratitude trap (according to Ellen Kenner, a "deceptive" kindness used to make others feel indebted), always being right (a type of personalization in which being wrong is simply inconceivable), fallacy of change (another personalization distortion characterized by the belief that one's happiness depends on others, and thus it's acceptable to pressure others to change, often present in abusive relationships) were identified and added to the body of knowledge.

Most cognitive distortions are bad news because they tend to make you waste your time and precious mental resources on them; they also affect your mood and interfere with problem-solving. All these really accomplish is making you less focused on your tasks.

A good way of regaining your focus is playing mental games. What are mental games? They are exercises for the brain, and they distract you from cognitive distortions. These are fun, quick exercises that present enough of a challenge to engage you and get you back to working on the important things in no time. Don't worry if you don't like mental challenges or puzzles. They shouldn't be too difficult to the point of making you frustrated. Ideally, they should last no more than two minutes. Let's go over the list of games:

- **Math (1)**: It is time to recollect your second-grade days by reviewing the multiplication table. Bonus challenge: try to finish the whole multiplication table in under two minutes!
- **Math (2)**: count backward starting from 1,000, but only in increments of seven. This one is interesting because it helps decrease acute pain by up to 50%, according to a study[20].
- **Song lyrics and poetry**: recite your favorite song lyrics or poem. Try to avoid sad songs, please. Do go for upbeat, optimistic, cheerful songs.
- **Flashback**: choose a pleasant memory and recall as many details as you can. Pretend this is a very short guided imagery exercise but for your fondest memories. For example, recollect all your school teachers' names, the places you've visited with your family, the layout of your childhood home, your favorite childhood TV shows, your first date, etc.
- **Shiritori**: This is a popular Japanese game that has been adapted to work with the English language. It's usually

played with two or more people, but you can do it by yourself. Come up with a word, and use its last letter to start a new word. No repeats are allowed. For example: (1) Cat, (2) Tailor, (3) Ruminate, (4) Elephant, (5) Taco, etc. You can increase the difficulty by selecting categories such as nouns, verbs, adjectives, animals, fruits, etc.

- **Categories**: name as many items in a chosen category as you can. Besides the categories mentioned above, you can use cocktails, legumes, vegetables, brands, artists, movies, etc. Make it harder by naming items in alphabetical order. Reverse the alphabetical order if it gets stale.
- **The ABC Game**: talking of alphabetical order, coming up with famous people's names for every pair of initials. For example: (AB) Adrien Brody, (BC) Bill Clinton, (CD) Charles Dickens, (DE) Dwight Eisenhower, etc. Make it harder by choosing a category beforehand, such as athletes, actors, Nobel prize winners, musicians, writers, and so on.

You're obviously not restricted to the games above. Come up with your own games, or search for more online. Mental games are pretty good at making you focus on something else besides negative thought patterns. But they aren't the only ones. You can play games to distract yourself. Sudoku, chess, crossword puzzles, and wordle are just a few examples. Mobile phone games, or their clearly superior counterparts, the console and PC games, can also be used for that purpose, provided they're appropriate for the situation.

Remember: Every time you find yourself in an emotionally challenging situation, use the techniques above to slow down and regain some balance. When the intensity of those emotions decreases, and when you have a moment, use the scientific method or detecting **iceberg beliefs** to understand why you're reacting the way you did. Once you know more about the situation, you can decide if the belief is helpful or unhelpful.

Real-time Resilience

This skill is as effective as the previous techniques for calming yourself down. The advantage of this skill versus the previous ones is that it helps you change your beliefs on a deeper level as they occur. With time and lots of practice, you'll notice that the quantity and the intensity of those unhelpful thoughts will be decreased.

The objective of this skill is to change those non-resilient thoughts into a more accurate version of themselves. You're not trying to change them to pie-in-the-sky, positive thoughts. Instead, what you want is to increase your comprehension of the situation, no matter how complex it may seem. Once you have a better understanding of the adversity, you can focus on planning the best way forward.

You need to come up with rational responses to your unhelpful beliefs now. You need three things: **alternatives**, **evidence**, and **implications**.

- **Alternatives**: A good way of generating an accurate alternative to your belief is to finish the statement, "A more accurate way of seeing this situation is..." For example, you have the belief that "My presentation will crash and burn, and my boss will never give me a project to lead." Create an alternative belief by saying, "A more accurate way of seeing this situation is that I'll be nervous at the beginning, but the presentation will go according to plan because I rehearsed dozens of times and know the subject very well."
- **Evidence**: Question the accuracy of your belief by using the phrase "that's not true because..." and come up with evidence to the contrary of your current belief. The main issue when looking for evidence to disprove your belief is confirmation bias, "people's tendency to process information by looking for or interpreting information that is consistent with their

existing beliefs"[21]. When you start your answer with "that's not true because..." you can avoid confirmation bias. An example: "My brother is a selfish jerk! He only cares about himself and loves to belittle me." But is this really true? Let's see: "That's not true because he calls me on my birthday every year and always asks if I need anything. He also always sends a Christmas card, except when he got really sick and was rushed to a hospital."

- **Implications**: Many people tend to focus only on the worst-case scenarios related to their unhealthy beliefs. Generally speaking, in order to counter this tendency, psychologists advise their patients to come up with a worst-case scenario, then a best-case scenario, and finally, a likely outcome. This is a great way to counter your beliefs, but depending on the situation, you might not have the luxury of some peace and quiet. That's why you can start your questioning with a realistic outcome and subsequently come up with one way you can deal with it. And you do that by saying, "A more likely outcome is... and I can... to deal with it." Here's an example: "My boyfriend is gonna dump me, and I won't be able to get over the breakup and will probably never find someone who loves me, warts and all." Now, this person can answer this belief with, "A more likely outcome is that we will have a serious conversation, and if we really break up, then I can focus on my career, my hobbies, and my friends, take some time to heal, and get back to the dating scene when I'm ready."

Now, like everything related to mental health, it takes some practice to use these three items quickly and effectively. You'll probably make mistakes along the way, and that's fine. How else are you going to learn without making mistakes? How can you expect to succeed without failing? Without mistakes or failures, we stand to gain nothing. So consider them part of the process. There are four main mistakes that may make things worse.

The first mistake when engaging in this questioning is: being too optimistic. That's a common problem, especially when looking for alternatives to your beliefs. What we want are accurate, realistic alternatives. That means not lying to yourself. Be honest: Are you trying to produce happy, unrealistic alternatives out of thin air so that you can be done with this exercise? If the alternative you came up with sounded superficial or unnatural, then you had better give it a bit more thought. There's nothing wrong with being optimistic. It's a good thing when associated with self-efficacy. Just try not to delude yourself in the process. Here's an example of a presentation: "My presentation will crash and burn, and my boss will never give me a project to lead." An overly optimistic response would be, "A more accurate way of seeing this is that my presentation will be overwhelmingly good, the feedback forms will be full of praise, and my boss will not only ask me to lead an important project but will also recommend me to the director for a promotion."

The second mistake that people make is: engaging in minimization. Minimization doesn't exclusively mean that you disregard the positive parts of an experience; it can mean disregarding risks or the importance of events in your life. Minimization is especially common when trying to understand the implications of a belief and creating a course of action. Using the example from the implications part above: "My boyfriend is gonna dump me, and I won't be able to get over the breakup, and will probably never find someone who loves me, warts and all."

Minimizing this situation would sound like this: "A more likely outcome is that we will have a serious conversation, and I'll do my best to listen to his complaints. Then I can focus on doing everything he'd like me to do and stop doing the things he hates." Uh, no, sorry to break it to you, but you are not only minimizing the important bits of that belief, but you're also downright enforcing the need for acceptance, a very common **iceberg belief.** Being dumped is pretty devastating, but it's not the end of the world. People get over it all the time. Why wouldn't you?

The third common mistake is: minimizing the truth. Sometimes, your assessment of a situation has an element of truth to it. This will often happen when you're trying to refute your unhelpful thinking patterns with evidence. Revisiting that example from the evidence bullet point: "My brother is a selfish jerk! He only cares about himself and loves to belittle me." You looked for evidence to the contrary and found that your brother calls you on your birthday and pretty consistently sends Christmas cards. But then you remember all the times your brother made fun of you in front of the whole family while praising your other brother even when he didn't deserve it. What about all the instances when your brother had said he would take your mother to her medical appointment only to cancel at the last minute with a silly excuse such as having to play golf with his boss? The difficult part here is to see the truth that your brother is not always completely bad or completely good. Another challenge is to do something to improve the situation, like having a heart-to-heart conversation with him.

The fourth and final mistake, called the blame game, is related to personalization. It's the action of either believing you are to blame for everything or believing that others are responsible for misfortunes. This cognitive distortion is very easy to overlook. If you notice a tendency to do either type of personalization, be aware that just reversing the belief doesn't mean you'll automatically have a deeper understanding of the situation and will be able to affect change. Just because you started pointing fingers at others when you tend to blame yourself, it doesn't mean it's the same as an effective rebuttal. Conversely, blaming yourself for others' shortcomings or misguided behavior won't improve your mental health.

In the beginning, when you start using the resources above, that is, coming up with alternatives, evidence, and likely outcomes, use the sentences taught to better structure your answers. Dig deep for evidence, don't just create unrealistic, illogical phrases that don't really add anything substantial. To help with that, imagine you're a lawyer or a researcher: would you accept questionable evidence? Then, find something substantial. When you feel more confident, use the best ones for you. No need to use all three types every single time. Just be careful with the four common mistakes.

Key Takeaways

- The scientific method is a way to question your beliefs, actions, and emotions, especially when facing adversities.
- The scientific method consists of six steps designed to help you question your irrational beliefs. They are: observe, hypothesize, be skeptical, test it, question the merit, and keep your goals and standards in mind.
- The ABCDE method is another version of the **ABC model** used to fight your irrational beliefs. It is designed to help you effect real change.
- Ellis' main irrational beliefs are: awfulizing, horribleizing, and terribleizing; perfectionism and grandiosity; worthlessness and self-hatred; self-damnation and undeservingness; low frustration tolerance (*I can't-stand-it-itis*); and belief in totality, allness, and neverness.
- Fast skills allow you to calm down quickly and regain your focus when you don't want to use the ABCDE. They're divided into two categories: **relaxing techniques** (**4-7-8**, **4-4-4-4**, **three-part breathing**, **PMR**, **mindfulness**, and **guided imagery**) and **focusing techniques** (mental games).
- Real-time resilience is another method for rationally responding to unhelpful, irrational beliefs. For that, you need **alternatives**, **evidence**, and **implications**.
- When using real-time resilience, there are four main mistakes to avoid: being too optimistic, minimization, minimizing the truth, and the blame game.

And now we end chapter 3. In the next chapter, we'll discuss how what we have discussed so far can be practical in the main parts of our lives.

---

1. Albert Ellis. *How to Stubbornly Refuse to Make Yourself Miserable About Anything-yes, Anything!* Kensington Publishing Corp. New York, NY. 2006.
2. Goyal Rajni, Hem Lata, Lily Walia, and Manjit K Narula. "Effect of pranayama on rate pressure product in mild hypertensives." *Int J Appl Basic Med Res.* 2014 Jul;4(2):67-71.
3. Novaes, Morgana M, Fernanda Palhano-Fontes, Heloisa Onias, Katia C Andrade, Bruno Lobão-Soares, Tiago Arruda-Sanchez, Elisa H Kozasa, Danilo F Santaella, Draulio B de Araujo. "Effects of Yoga Respiratory Practice (Bhastrika pranayama) on Anxiety, Affect, and Brain Functional Connectivity and Activity: A Randomized Controlled Trial." *Front Psychiatry.* 2020 May 21;11:467.
4. Shastri, Vasant V, Alex Hankey, Bhawna Sharma, and Sanjib Patra. "Investigation of Yoga Pranayama and Vedic Mathematics on Mindfulness, Aggression and Emotion Regulation." *International Journal of Yoga.* 2017 Sep-Dec;10(3):138-144.
5. Shankarappa V, Prashanth P, Annamalai P, and Malhotra V."The Short Term Effect of Pranayama on the Lung Parameters." *Journal of Clinical and Diagnostic Research.* 2012 February, 15. Vol-6(1): 27-30.
6. Shahab, Lion, Bidyut K Sarkar, and Robert West. "The Acute Effects of Yogic Breathing Exercises on Craving and Withdrawal Symptoms in Abstaining Smokers." *Psychopharmacology* (Berl). 2013 Feb;225(4):875-82.
7. Andrew Weil, "Breathing Exercises: Three to Try," *DrWeil.com*, https://www.drweil.com/videos-features/videos/breathing-exercises-three-to-try/.
8. Edmund Jacobson, *Progressive Relaxation: A Physiological and Clinical Investigation of Muscular States and Their Significance in Psychology and Medical Practice* (Chicago: University of Chicago Press, 1938)
9. Harorani, Mehdi, Fahimeh Davodabady, Behnam Masmouei, and Niloofar Barati. "The effect of progressive muscle relaxation on anxiety and sleep quality in burn patients: A randomized clinical trial." *Burns*, 2020 Volume 46, Issue 5, Pages 1107-1113.
10. Sheu, Sheila, Barbara L Irvin, Huey-Shyan Lin, and Chun-Lin Mar. "Effects of progressive muscle relaxation on blood pressure and psychosocial status for clients with essential hypertension in Taiwan." *Holist Nurs Pract.* 2003 Jan-Feb;17(1):41-7.
11. Meyer, Bianca, Armin Keller, Hans-Georg Wöhlbier, Claudia H Overath, Britta Müller, and Peter Kropp. "Progressive muscle relaxation reduces migraine frequency and normalizes amplitudes of contingent negative variation (CNV)." *J Headache Pain.* 2016;17:37.

12. Mateu, Margarita, Olga Alda, Maria-Del-Mar Inda, Cesar Margarit, Raquel Ajo, Domingo Morales, Carlos J van-der Hofstadt, and Ana M Peiró. "Randomized, Controlled, Crossover Study of Self-administered Jacobson Relaxation in Chronic, Nonspecific, Low-back Pain." *Altern Ther Health Med.* 2018 Nov; 24(6):22-30.

13. Merakou, Kyriakoula, Konstantinos Tsoukas, Giorgio Stavrinos, Eirini Amanaki, Antonia Daleziou, Ntina Kourmousi, Georgia Stamatelopoulou, Evi Spourdalaki, and Anastasia Barbouni. "The Effect of Progressive Muscle Relaxation on Emotional Competence: Depression-Anxiety-Stress, Sense of Coherence, Health-Related Quality of Life, and Well-Being of Unemployed People in Greece: An Intervention Study." *Explore* (NY). 2019 Jan-Feb;15(1):38-46.

14. Dusek, J. A., et al. "Stress Management Versus Lifestyle Modification on Systolic Hypertension and Medication Elimination: a Randomized Trial." *J Altern Complement Med.* 2008 Mar;14(2):129-38.

15. Davidson, R. J., et al. "Alterations in Brain and Immune Function Produced by Mindfulness Meditation." *Psychosomatic Medicine* 65, no. 4 (2003): 564–570.

16. Lin, Yanli, William D Eckerle, Ling W Peng, and Jason S Moser. 2019. "On Variation in Mindfulness Training: A Multimodal Study of Brief Open Monitoring Meditation on Error Monitoring" *Brain Sciences* 9, no. 9: 226.

17. Whitfield, T., et al. "The Effect of Mindfulness-based Programs on Cognitive Function in Adults: A Systematic Review and Meta-analysis." *Neuropsychology Review* 32, no. 3 (2022): 677–702.

18. Basso, Julia C., Mathias McHale, Lisa Ende, Emily L. Oberlin, and Wendy A. Suzuki. "Brief, Daily Meditation Enhances Attention, Memory, Mood, and Emotional Regulation in Non-experienced Meditators." *Behavioural Brain Research* 356 (2019): 208-220.

19. Cleveland Clinic. "Guided Imagery: How It Helps With Stress & Managing Anxiety." *Cleveland Clinic Health Essentials*, September 13, 2022. https://health.clevelandclinic.org/guided-imagery-how-it-helps-with-stress-managing-anxiety/.

20. Schulz, Enrico, Anne Stankewitz, Anderson M Winkler, Stephanie Irving, Viktor Witkovský, and Irene Tracey. "Ultra-high-field imaging reveals increased whole brain connectivity underpins cognitive strategies that attenuate pain." *eLife.* 2020 Sep 2;9:e55028.

21. "Confirmation Bias." *Encyclopedia Britannica*, January 2023.

Chapter Four

Practical Application of Mental Resilience

> Although the world is full of suffering, it is also full of the overcoming of it.
>
> —Hellen Keller, author and educator

It's time to look at examples of mental resilience in the main spheres of everyday life. This is not an exhaustive list by any means. I'll focus on work, marriage and long-term relationships, and life in general.

Mental Resilience for Work

Have you wondered how many hours people in your country work in a year, on average? The OECD, the Organisation for Economic Co-operation and Development, collects data from its participating members to plot trends over time. The latest data might surprise you. The country that works the least is Germany, with 1,341 hours worked. Colombia is on the other side of the chart, with 2,405. The United States currently sits at 1,811 hours, while Japan is at 1,607 hours[1].

I should point out that the OECD website makes it clear in the abstract that "Actual hours worked include regular work hours of full-time, part-time and part-year workers, paid and unpaid overtime, hours worked in additional jobs" So, no need to send me angry emails telling me people in your country work way more than the data presented in the website.

All right, now you have an idea of how much people work. No wonder everybody is stressed out all the time—we work too much! The reality is that work is a very big part of our lives, and for some of us, it encroaches on our rest and recuperation. The skills this book teaches will allow you to see the adversities you encounter in your career more accurately. This doesn't mean you'll find everlasting happiness in your work environment. I wish! Instead, you'll be able to operate like a true stoic philosopher when you face the loss of a job, prejudice in the workplace, problems with work-life balance, a toxic company culture, and excessive demands with few available resources.

Unemployment

This topic is a tough one. It creates a lot of uncertainties, stress, and anxiety. I should know, as all the employees on my team and I got laid off while I was writing this book. As soon as I heard the news, all kinds of crazy thoughts and emotions came rushing in. I experienced a large dose of catastrophizing and arbitrary inference. I had to use almost all the techniques in this book to return to a balanced state of mind. Maybe you have personally experienced being fired and the emotional state that entailed. If not, let me tell you upfront: it's not fun. Unemployment is even more destabilizing if you have a family that depends on you, a student loan, and a mortgage.

To maintain a semblance of sanity, you had better be accurate and flexible when thinking about why you got fired and the associated beliefs (as well as the **iceberg beliefs**, if any). This will help you think about how to solve your main problem i.e. unemployment.

Let's go through a few techniques I used upon hearing the bad news.

ABC Technique

Among the jumble of thoughts I experienced, one was particularly tough to handle and kept coming back in an endless loop. Here's how I dealt with it:

Adversity*:* I got fired from my company last week.

Belief*:* I'll never find a better job with the same benefits and pay, especially in this economy (What-next belief). I must find a job, but most jobs pay much less than what I make. I just hate the idea of doing things I'd rather not do and having to take a pay cut, and this shows how ridiculously messed up the current labor market is (hot, irrational thoughts).

Consequences*:* Feeling intense anxiety and intense shame (emotional consequences); complained to everyone within earshot distance about being laid off and stopped looking for jobs online (behavioral consequences).

In a situation like this, feeling anxiety is completely normal. It relates to the future. But what about the shame? Wouldn't anger be more appropriate? After all, a company that lays off its employees effectively deprives them of an income, affecting their survival and mental balance.

If you look back at the table in Chapter 2, shame is associated with comparison to others in a negative light. How is that even remotely related to losing a job? This tells us that there is a disconnect between the beliefs and the consequences. And when we have a disconnect, that could mean **iceberg beliefs** are at play here.

Do you remember how to deal with **iceberg beliefs**? We question them using the keyword "What...?" Here are the questions I asked myself in trying to understand the hidden beliefs:

Belief: "I must find a job, but most jobs pay much less than what I make. I just hate the idea of doing things I'd rather not do and having to take a pay cut."

Question: "What's so bad about that?"

Answer: "It's bad because I don't want to go back to being just a low-level teacher. That means not only taking a huge pay cut, but also working long, odd hours, and performing tasks not directly related to teaching."

Question: "What does that say about me?"

Answer: "It feels like I should be able to get a job with the responsibilities and the pay appropriate to my age and experience. If I can't get that, I'll be back at square one, working at an entry-level job usually reserved for new grads."

Question: "What's the most upsetting part of that for me?"

Answer: "It's pretty clear what it means: that I don't have the necessary skills to make progress in my career. It means that I'm actually regressing. How would my friends and family treat me if they learned I'm back at teaching weeknights and weekends and couldn't spend time with them?"

When I asked those questions, I got two insights into my hidden beliefs. First, I had a need for achievement, represented by the desire to advance my career, and second, I had a need for acceptance, represented by better pay and status. The matter of the fact was that neither would be achievable—at least not at that moment. Looking at others with the same experience and skills and at the same age, I should be able to get a better job. Clearly, I wasn't. Thus, I felt shame rather than anger.

Doing nothing about this situation was not going to help me find a job. Since the current labor market is paying peanuts to experienced professionals in several sectors, I figured that taking a pay cut was unavoidable at the moment. I came to the conclusion that not improving my current skills or learning new ones would be silly. I also thought that maybe a career change could be an interesting challenge. I then set out to get certificates online from two famous websites. That way, I could start learning new things and get ready for beginner-level, industry-recognized certifications such as CompTIA A+ and PMP, should I decide to fork out the necessary cash. This lecture was just to illustrate the power of questioning yourself: once you see what's happening, you're in a better condition to improve your feelings and your behavior.

Prejudice in The Workplace

The skills you've learned throughout the book can be used to deal with prejudice and the emotions that arise when experiencing discrimination.

Now, the tricky part is determining whether you're experiencing real prejudice or whether you're buying into your own bias. How can you know if it's prejudice when dealing with situations in the workplace? You don't. You can't read minds. The only way to be sure is to have a racist comment directed at you, like a joke or demeaning terms and expressions.

So, how do we handle this ambiguity? Besides working on your mental resilience, you could take a more practical approach, depending on the country you live in. It's hard to fight prejudice in the workplace without evidence, so document everything regarding the incident, such as date, time, who was present, what was said, and what the general reaction of those involved was, as well as anything that might be relevant. Don't forget to save those notes somewhere safe. Remember, though, that your company's desktop/laptop computer, your desk drawer, or your locker are not safe places to store the information. After that, read up on your company's policies and/or employee handbook. That way, you learn what needs to be done in terms of formalizing a complaint. Remember to maintain records throughout the whole process. If you have the means, contact a lawyer sooner rather than later. Depending on your company's policies, you might have to make official complaints to your company's HR department, but do keep in mind that HR is there to protect the company against the employees, not the other way around. Study the local and national labor laws pertinent to your country and contact the appropriate institutions. Throughout the process, you should think about what you want out of this ordeal. If the company is unwilling to make the necessary changes, ask yourself: "Do I want to stay in a place like this?"

Now, getting back to the issue at hand: mental resilience in the workplace. If you face an ambiguous situation, pay attention to what kind of belief is present and the consequences that follow. If the consequences don't match the beliefs, then **iceberg beliefs** may be in operation. Use any technique taught in this book that you find effective when you notice irrational beliefs erupting. If breathing deeply is enough to make you slow down and regain emotional balance, do it. Or, if you prefer to use mental games, go right ahead. Keep in mind that just because someone made insensitive or downright racist comments to you, it doesn't mean that person is completely bad. You are allowed to feel anger, frustration, or other negative feelings. But try to keep them in the "healthy" category (before you ask, I do have experience living in Japan as a foreigner for over thirteen years. I met a lot of wonderful people, but I've also had my fair share of prejudice directed at me).

Work-Life Balance

The COVID-19 pandemic gave a whole new meaning to work-life balance. Of course, not everyone was positively affected by this shift in paradigm. But it allowed for new ways of working to become more prominent, such as the four-day work week, remote work, the hybrid model of working, the increased reliance on hot-desking, among others.

Work-life balance, the ability to juggle work and non-work tasks and needs, can be understood as a necessary skill for mental resilience. People have different kinds of relationships with work. Some love it and become true workaholics, deriving meaning and motivation from it. Others view it as a means to survive or maintain their habits and hobbies. Whatever your relationship with work, you might have struggled to keep your work and your life outside of it apart. Doing the **ABCDE** analysis is a good start if you have problems deciding which is more important.

Let's imagine that your mother is sick, and you can't afford to have her move into a nursing home. Every time she feels unwell, it makes you worried about her, and you're the only one able to take care of her, so you try your best to take her to the clinic.

Your boss, however, is not happy with the frequent time-off requests and has made it clear that this situation is unacceptable. You understand how delicate the situation is but are reluctant to choose between family and work since both are important to you.

The **ABCDE** analysis could go like this:

Adversity*:* I need to take my mom to the clinic, but my boss is not happy about this situation. He said he would no longer accept this.

Belief*:* This company is not as accommodating as they made me believe five years ago when I joined. What happened to the 'we care about work-life balance?' Haven't I paid my dues with the unpaid overtime and successful project landings? Now that I really need the so-called balance, they grant a few days but immediately tell me it's not okay? They should keep their promise and let me take care of my mother.

Consequences*:* Feeling intense anxiety about my mother's health, and intense anger (the emotional consequences); dragged my feet the whole day and started looking for better jobs online (the behavioral consequences).

Dispute*:* Where is it written that they should cater to my personal needs?

Effective New Philosophy*:* Nowhere. They have their policies, and they have to follow labor laws. If I accept work overtime without getting paid, that's on me. They did pay me very good bonuses over the past three years. My boss granted every time-off request I made to look after my mother in the past six months without following procedure. That shows me that he understands my situation. It's possible that his boss took notice of the situation and pressured him to put a lid on it. The way out of this situation is to either see if the department can implement a flex-time scheme or look for a job that fits my situation.

Please keep in mind that everybody has a different situation when working on your work-life balance. So, conduct your own **ABCDE** analysis to create new rational beliefs that lead to behaviors aligned with your life goals.

Toxic Company Culture

What is company or corporate culture? The answer is, in simple terms, the beliefs held collectively in a work environment. Just like people have all different kinds of beliefs—some rational, some irrational—so do companies have them. And just like people behave in certain ways because of their beliefs, companies (their employees, actually) behave in specific ways, influenced by their own beliefs.

According to Atlassian, an Australian software company, a toxic culture in a company or team means "little to no enthusiasm, pervasive fear of failure, constant confusion and dysfunction, never-ending gossip and drama, and high employee turnover."[2] Forbes, a business publication established in 1917, has a similar list: "Hustle culture (represented by long work hours and little return), blame culture (and 'every worker for themselves' mentality), clique culture, authoritative culture, and fear-based culture."[3] You can probably see the kind of problems a toxic work culture can create not only for the productivity of a team but also for an employee's wellbeing.

Changing corporate culture is a task for upper management, but that doesn't mean you can't influence how you feel, behave, and think while working in a toxic workplace.

The first step is to recognize that the corporate culture is toxic. Look for the signs of toxicity mentioned in the previous paragraph. Now, look at your behaviors inside the company, compare them against your values, and ask yourself if you're part of the problem. Do you tend to make snide remarks when others make mistakes? Are you bullying others and blaming the victims to justify your behavior? If you were to ask yourself, *Do I lack empathy?* What would be the answer?

The second step is to ensure you're not carrying around irrational beliefs. Conduct an ABC analysis if you find beliefs that do not support your goal for happiness and job satisfaction. Work on changing those beliefs into helpful, rational ones via any technique you see fit. If you find **iceberg beliefs**, asking for evidence won't help you, as most hidden beliefs represent values. In that case, ask if holding those beliefs is helpful or not.

The third step is to make a decision: are you going to look for a different job, or are you going to stay and try to change your company's culture? If you choose the latter, you could start by talking with someone in HR or a leader in the company who can affect change. Provide data with examples of the toxic culture in action to get your point across. Consider making a group with other employees who agree that the toxic culture has to change and talk to upper management. If management is open to suggestions, offer to create a task force. Be aware that the toxicity may be so entrenched that upper management may not consider it a problem; they may label you a troublemaker and even retaliate. Be ready.

Excessive Demands with Few Available Resources

Dealing with excessive demands with few resources creates a lot of stress for employees. In this economy, some companies expect project managers and project members to provide high-quality deliverables with scarce resources or make changes to projects' scope without changing budget or schedule. What a recipe for disaster.

The best way to deal with stress in those situations is to use the skills discussed in the previous chapter, such as breathing techniques or progressive muscle relaxation. Practicing **mindfulness** every day, for five to ten minutes a day, is a very good start. Don't forget to inventory all the irrational beliefs that pop up so you can deal with them accordingly. Pay special attention to any shoulds or musts and work on disputing them.

When you get a clearer picture of the beliefs and consequences related to work, see if there are no issues with time management, prioritization of tasks, proper task delegation to team members, and an excessive number of meetings—this one depends on several factors, but why have a meeting when an email would suffice?

Need more actionable advice? Here is a list adapted from the Harvard Business Review, Forbes Health, and the American Psychological Association websites[4, 5, 6]:

1. **Document your work-related sources of stress for two weeks**: This is an **ABC** analysis. Write down the adversities, the beliefs, and the consequences.

2. **Develop a healthy response to your stressors**: Going for a walk, listening to your favorite song, meditating, hitting the gym, playing a mobile game, studying a language, and calling your parents are all good ways of dealing with stress. If possible, set aside a specific time to do these activities, for example, right after your shift. If not possible, sit down for five minutes by your desk

and meditate or use guided imagery.

3. **Implement a break schedule: use a method, such as the pomodoro technique, to have breaks scattered throughout your work day**: Walk around, stretch, meditate, play a game, listen to a song, or anything that allows you to slow down.

4. **Create boundaries**: Everybody has different needs, so experiment with ways to detach from work, such as turning off your company smartphone, setting your phone to Do Not Disturb mode, implementing a no-phone-at-the-dinner-table rule, not answering the phone after a certain time of the day (e.g., 6 p.m.).

5. **Improve your sleep quality and health**: Make sure to fulfill your sleep needs in quantity and quality (for example, a dark and quiet room, a cold environment, the right mattress, etc.). Don't forget to find a pleasant physical activity that allows you to do it long-term and improve your health simultaneously. If you prefer to work on your garden instead of running, go for it.

6. **Talk to your manager**: Discuss the sources of stress you've identified and come up with a plan to handle them together. Try not to just make complaints, work on ideas to resolve them. Keep in mind that not every company nor every manager will be willing to work with you or have the necessary resources to deal with those issues.

7. **Get support**: Involve your friends and family members in your stress management efforts. Getting professional help from a mental health therapist, a psychologist, or a psychiatrist can be incredibly useful. If your company has the necessary resources, such as stress relief programs or other related employee assistance programs, make sure to utilize them.

One more thing: remember to focus on things that you can control rather than the ones you can't. Also, your worth as a human being is not directly tied to the quality of your work.

Resilience in Marriage and Long-term Relationships

In terms of relationships, two main things can end an otherwise stable relationship: lack of communication and fighting. Of course, fighting, no matter the scale, is an expected part of living with someone. Lack of communication, on the other hand, is *the* death knell that couples should be careful about. The objective of this section is to provide tools so couples can better communicate. And if they have to fight, then they will do it effectively so they can strengthen their relationship.

Keep in mind that relationships end in spite of your best efforts. The pain can be emotionally excruciating, as anyone who has ever been through a breakup will tell you. The outcome of such events will reflect your resilience: will you mourn, hold a grudge, or move on? How long will it take for you to overcome these emotions?

Factors that lead to a separation in a relationship are very similar to the ones that lead to divorce. Besides lack of communication and fighting, lack of sex, friendship, and variety are the other big ones. Some others, for example, financial literacy, religious backgrounds, divorced parents, and marrying at a very young age, are factors out of your control and are very difficult to reverse once they set in. But do you know what can be changed and is possible to control? Communication and the way you fight.

Dr. Howard Markman, together with co-authors Scott Stanley and Susan Blumberg, in their book *Fighting for Your Marriage*[7], defined four sets of beliefs and their emotions—called filters—that distort the messages between partners and hamper good communication, leading to problems. If you immediately thought of bias or other cognitive distortions when I mentioned filters, then pat yourself on the back because you were very close.

Here's the list:

- **Attention level**: When your partner converses with you, are you paying attention? Are you totally focused on what he/she is saying? If not, then obviously, communication is going to suffer. Maybe you're distracted thinking about a tight deadline for an important project. Or maybe you're just really focused on the latest episode of that show that got uploaded to your favorite streaming service. Perhaps you can't focus on your partner due to other environmental sources of distraction. Slow breathing and other focusing techniques help with this filter.

- **Beliefs**: Any time you start a conversation, including the ones with your partner, you bring beliefs created throughout the day to it. That means adversities, positive situations, and other conversations will influence this second filter. How do you think a discussion with your significant other would go after your retirement fund took a beating and depreciated by thirty percent? How about if your boss gave you a verbal warning in front of your team? It probably wouldn't go very well. Some jumping to conclusions or mind-reading thought patterns might creep in and break communication down even further. Whatever the problem, it's important to pay attention to and dispute your irrational beliefs.

- **Feelings**: Depending on the feelings and emotions you are experiencing during the conversation, your interpretation of what's being said can be distorted negatively by those emotions. Try to keep a cool head and, if you need to, gently tell your partner that you need some time out before continuing with the conversation. Use that opportunity to calm yourself down and question your beliefs with the scientific method or the three items from the real-time resilience section: alternatives, evidence, and implications.

- **Communication styles:** couples sometimes have different communication styles. Some people love to share their emotions, some others prefer to keep to themselves, others may prefer action rather than words, etc. Having different communication styles is fine, expected even, unless it causes problems in the relationship. If it does, then **iceberg beliefs** might be the source of the problems, as your communication style is often a byproduct of your hidden beliefs. I'll go over how to work on your **iceberg beliefs** later in this section.

The best way to deal with the four filters above is to be alert to their presence and work toward open communication without going ballistic.

Here's a short list you can follow:

- If something your partner says pushes your buttons, recognize it and ask for a time-out. Once you're alone, use the **ABC** (or the **ABCDE**) **method** to reframe the situation.

- If you notice any cognitive distortion in the conversation (such as black-and-white thinking, jumping to conclusions, or personalization), dispute them as best you can. Alternatively, ask your partner whether your situation assessment is correct without flying off the handle.

- Test the accuracy of your beliefs by adopting a questioning posture, like the questions we discussed in the **iceberg beliefs** section of Chapter 2. You can also ask yourself the three questions in the real-time resilience section of Chapter 3: "A more accurate way of seeing this situation is..." "That's not true because..." and "A more likely outcome is... and I can... to deal with it."

- When communication starts to break down because either of you can't change your mood, even after using the techniques mentioned, remember again how to uncover hidden beliefs and the standard Belief-Consequence pairs discussed in Chapter 2. If something you said triggered anger in your partner, talk it out and find out why they are angry rather than say embarrassed or anxious. Remember, when the consequence doesn't match with the belief, then **iceberg beliefs** may explain these feelings. Asking *what* questions rather than *why* questions will help you dig deeper and lead to a better understanding.

Remember to work on each other's irrational beliefs together, perhaps taking turns or returning to the subject at another opportunity. Also, don't expect the first few conversations to go smoothly. They will feel very uncomfortable at first. You just need to keep at it until you develop some proficiency.

Fighting is the other key factor that leads to breakups. And to be absolutely clear, fighting *does not* involve slapping, punching, kicking, or hitting your significant other. If that's how you fight with your partner, you need psychological help. Fighting doesn't involve emotional or psychological abuse either—or, at least, it shouldn't. Research and contact the appropriate helpline in your area if you need support.

When talking about fights, I'm referring to arguments. There are several different styles of fighting, but they can all be slotted into two main types: the "**What's wrong with you?**" and the "**Whose side are you on?**"

The **"What's wrong with you?"** is a combative, scathing, and condemnatory fight. Imagine being criticized for a small mistake or something innocuous that triggers you, and you blurt something out, such as, "Really? Did you decide that doing this now was a good time? You know we cannot be late for our appointment! What's wrong with you? Why do you always have to be so oblivious in the worst possible moments?" or something similar designed to hurt your partner's feelings.

The "**Whose side are you on?**" is a healthy way of fighting. Its objective is to understand and resolve the issue at hand, keeping the complaints specific and free from ambiguity. It is not designed to poke your partner but to urge him/her into inquiry mode. We'll discuss how to do that in a moment.

Hurting your significant other's feelings so you can get a temporary ego boost while thinking *that'll show him/her* is far from healthy and will just damage your relationship. It's important to point out that almost all couples will experience difficult times, whether they're disagreements and arguments or tragedies outside their control. Independent of the type of adversity, relationships require effort and patience to work. Being understanding and having a desire to work things out without abuse or violence is the resilient way of fighting.

There are two main things you should be aware of and try to avoid when fighting: caustic beginnings and character assassination. These two things, according to Dr. John Gottman in his book *The Seven Principles for Making Marriage Work*[8], are the big ones that predict divorce.

Caustic beginnings are when you start an argument that demeans and criticizes your spouse (also called a "harsh start-up"), often leading to a counter-argument with the same intensity and vitriol. All this achieves is hurt feelings rather than problem-solving or empathy. Signs of caustic beginnings include "you're such an..." and always-or-never statements loaded with sarcasm and irony. Once the conversation starts with caustic beginnings, it's very hard to pivot to a productive discussion.

Resist the desire to make a statement that might cause harm and humiliation at the beginning of an argument. Additionally, starting an argument with passive-aggressive statements will help neither of you, even if that means there are no raised voices, shouting, or profanity. If you believe that you have to start a fight with a caustic beginning, otherwise your partner will just disregard your concerns, think again. That in itself is an irrational belief. And you already know the power such beliefs have on our behaviors.

Moving on to character assassination. Simply put, you're engaging in character assassination when you criticize your partner's character rather than the offending behavior. Overgeneralization is often part of the equation because the accuser is effectively lumping the behavior together with the character—every mistake and offense is understood as a reflection of a defective character. It's like questioning whether your partner is worth the air they breathe but to their face. Not nice.

The trick to avoiding character assassination is to be deliberate in your criticisms by focusing on what can be changed. Behaviors, as you know, can be changed. The more specific you are, the better and healthier your fights will become. Even if the complaints on your part start with a "what's wrong with you?" kind of statement, as long as they focus on a behavior that can be changed, the fight will be healthier and may lead to resolution. An example would be, "What's with you? You've been complaining about the trip all day long," where the complaining behavior can be changed.

There are two main types of problems that couples fight about: **solvable problems** and **perpetual problems**. Dr. Gottman argues that if the fights are about specific issues and the events surrounding them are controllable, then a solution is often possible, provided the couple has a healthy style of fighting (no character assassination and no caustic beginnings). The other type of problem, the **perpetual** kind, is not as easy to solve because it involves fundamental personality differences. These differences, like introversion/extraversion, financial preferences, communication styles, or cleanliness/tidiness needs, are unlikely to change. These issues, as the name implies, are likely to happen time and again and may lead to what the author refers to as a "**gridlock**." That's right, the couple goes over the same issues and has the same complaints but makes no progress toward a resolution whatsoever. The kinds of problems couples face are usually of a perpetual variety, and when they reach a gridlock, the relationship usually starts to suffer. Feelings of rejection, hostility, exhaustion, and an unwillingness to compromise are common outcomes.

Use the **ABC** (or **ABCDE**) **method** to put your beliefs about your relationship and its problems into perspective. Look for thinking traps such as overgeneralization, black-or-white thinking, and mind-reading. Question everything and try to find rational alternatives. Then, discuss with your partner so you can find solutions together. Tired of having to do all the house chores by yourself? What kind of beliefs are at play here? Is it because your partner doesn't like cleaning? Is it because they never learned how to do it from their parents? Talk with your partner to understand the problem and find a solution together. Maybe you could make a list of all the chores, put them on a spreadsheet or piece of paper, and assign the tasks to the household members.

Is your partner not helping with the finances of the family? Why is that? Is the reason you came up with a rational or an irrational belief? What are the consequences? Anger? Sadness? Withdrawal? What evidence is there for those beliefs? Are there alternatives? Put your thoughts, feelings, and behaviors into paper, then discuss with your partner. Find solutions or compromises.

Let's return to the perpetual problems in a relationship. Remember that every relationship will have some kind of perpetual problem. You can do something about it, though. Take care not to allow your relationship to go too deep into a **gridlock**.

Signs of **gridlock**, according to Dr. Gottman, are:

- Saying the same things again and again.
- Unwillingness to compromise from both partners.
- Conflicts lead to feelings of rejection.
- Feelings of hostility and tiredness.

- Lack of generosity, humor, or empathy.
- Differences in perspective get exaggerated and become caricatured.

Look for **iceberg beliefs** that keep your relationship in a **gridlock**. I already mentioned a couple of examples of fundamental differences between partners (aka perpetual problems), so your job now is to understand how those differences are affecting your relationship and the hidden beliefs behind those problems.

As usual, a great way to start is to use the **ABC model**. Here's an example: you prefer the house clean and organized, while your partner doesn't mind hair and fur spread around the floor or upholstery. From your point of view, describe the problem, your beliefs, and the consequences.

- **Adversity**: "The house is a mess. There's hair and pet fur everywhere. My wife doesn't mind it, nor does she clean it."
- **Belief**: "What's the matter with her? Why not clean after herself and the pets? Do I have to keep cleaning it every day myself? I think it's because her mother did everything for her, being an only child and all."
- **Consequences**: "I clean the hair and pet fur myself. I become grumpy for having to do it every day and resent my wife for not helping more at home. Then I feel ashamed of the state of the house."

Grumpiness and resentment are associated with anger, indicating an infringement on rights, while shame is associated with being compared to others in a negative light. But this feels wrong, so you ask *what* questions to uncover hidden beliefs:

Question: What's so bad about her not cleaning the hair and fur?

Answer: That means she doesn't care about the state of the house.

Question: What makes that so upsetting?

Answer: Well, the house should be clean, at least presentable, in case we have an unexpected visit.

Question: Let's assume that the house is always dirty. What does that mean to you?

Answer: It means that it shouldn't be dirty. My mother taught me that a clean house is a mirror of our personalities. If it's dirty, then we are not nice people.

Well, I guess you can see the kind of insight this has provided: that we are bad people if our houses are dirty and that we are good people if our houses are clean. Talk about irrational beliefs. And a hidden one at that. With this insight, your spouse now understands that a clean house is important for you. She can now help you find a solution or compromise, decreasing the incidence of fights over the cleaning of the house. But before that, why not try to find out if there are any hidden beliefs or irrational ones on your spouse's side? That way, you not only get a better grasp of her inner workings but also engage in deep, meaningful conversation and understanding.

If, after many trials and tribulations, you used all the techniques you learned, and your relationship hasn't improved, you still have the option of talking to a professional, like a marriage counseling therapist. Keep in mind that therapists can only do so much to help you save your relationship. If you or your spouse don't put in the necessary effort to fix your issues, no matter how good or expensive your therapist is, you won't achieve the goal of working around your perpetual problems. Alternatively, the relationship may change, but not necessarily for the better for you or your significant other, for example.

If working with a professional hasn't yielded any of the results you or your partner hoped for, your relationship may have reached a dead end. And that can happen to anyone. Divorce (or a breakup) may feel like the end of the world. It will certainly be painful and sting every time you think about it after the fact. Being resilient won't affect the amount of pain you feel. Still, it will help you to move on, hopefully learning from the whole ordeal in the process (for example, understanding why it ended and what could be done better in a future relationship). Again, doing an **ABC** inventory after the separation can provide invaluable insight. After the breakup, your brain might come up with totally new and unexpected irrational beliefs, so do your best to use the techniques discussed in this book to dispute them and come up with new, healthy beliefs.

Here's a short list of common emotions after a difficult breakup or divorce:

- **Anger**: Recall that anger results from your rights being violated, and it's a very common response. It becomes a problem if it messes up other aspects of your life or if it slows down or halts your healing process. That anger can negatively affect your children and their relationship with the estranged parent. Yes, even though you're no longer together, your children still have a right to maintain a relationship with your ex-partner. Anger will often bring on cognitive distortions like minimization and magnification—you downplay the good things about your ex and magnify the negatives—and personalization in the form of blaming your ex for everything while playing the victim card. Put your anger and the associated beliefs in written form through an **ABC** process to make things easier. Then, work on disputing each irrational belief and cognitive distortion you find.
- **Sadness**: You might feel sad and even depressed after a difficult breakup. You probably know from past experiences how disruptive sadness can be in our day-to-day lives. A sense of loss or grief is usually the origin of your sadness or depression. You may also engage in some unhelpful thinking patterns, such as personalization, i.e., blaming yourself for the end of the relationship or thinking that there's something

wrong with you, making you incapable of having a healthy relationship. If it comes to that, think about it scientifically, questioning whether there's truth to those thoughts or not. If you need some order in all the chaos your brain creates after a separation, please use the **ABC method**. If the feeling of sadness can't be explained easily, that may mean that there are hidden beliefs. You know what to do: ask yourself *what* questions to dig them up.

- **Embarrassment or shame**: Both originate from being compared negatively to others. In terms of a divorce or breakup, you may think that you're responsible for the end of the relationship (a sign of personalization), that acquaintances and family members are feeling sorry for you (mind-reading), or that the end itself is a mirror of your flawed character or perhaps a personal failure that will haunt you forever. These then lead to feelings of embarrassment or shame. There is a chance that **iceberg beliefs** are creating those feelings, and you need to work on uncovering them to regain some balance and move on.

- **Anxiety**: Is the thought of having to date again or taking care of the kids all by yourself making you anxious? Or maybe your anxiety comes from the idea that you now have to take care of the finances or other important tasks that your ex used to help out with? Indeed, a breakup is capable of creating a lot of anxiety, and you may feel that even the smallest decision proves too difficult. Keeping your anxiety in check may be the best you can do, and that's okay. Remember that being resilient doesn't mean you won't feel any anxiety; it means you can handle it. The best way to lower your anxiety is to use any of the relaxing techniques we have discussed in Chapter 3, such as progressive muscle relaxation or breathing techniques. You can also come up with rational responses to your fears, in other words, alternatives, evidence, and implications. Work slowly on your irrational beliefs, and your anxiety will decrease.

- **Guilt**: Feeling guilty after a divorce is sometimes the natural consequence of the potential effects on your children. Or, if you were the one who ended the relationship, you may feel guilty because you may have hurt someone whom you have spent wonderful moments with. Either way, you may think the situation is worse than reality, which means you're probably engaging in catastrophizing. Alternatively, you may believe the end of your relationship was all on you, in which case you'd be personalizing the situation. Obviously, some guilt is normal, but if it's messing with your healing, you know you need to work on bringing it to a manageable level. You do that by using your trusty **ABC method** and working on each **Belief-Consequence** pair you find. If anything looks out of place, you need to uncover hidden beliefs.

Resilience for Life

The loss of a loved one is something indescribable. It feels as if something important has been ripped from deep inside you. We should all expect to experience this pain at some point in life. It's important to mention that certain events in life, such as the loss of someone dear to you, will create specific reactions. This is in direct contrast to the idea that our brain interprets events as the main motivator for our behaviors, thoughts, and feelings. Resilience here will only support you in connecting with friends and family members, which will help you with the grieving process.

Some people, when faced with the harsh reality that a loved one is not there anymore, will withdraw from their circle of friends and, sometimes, even from family members. That's part of the process. Feeling anger, pain, or depression are normal reactions that shouldn't be repressed. Being resilient in this respect is understanding that what you are feeling is natural. It also means remaining connected with other loved ones and continuing to live your life, even when emotions get in the way.

You can use real-time resilience when you feel irritated or upset with family members or friends who are trying their best to comfort you throughout the grieving process. Instead of thinking, "What was he thinking coming up with that stupid story about his wife? Hello? I just lost my wife to cancer! How can he be so insensitive?" try changing it to something akin to "All right, I understand he was trying to lighten the mood. He's trying his best to help me, given the situation. He's clearly embarrassed now, which shows that he cares." Taking a deep breath to slow things down will also help with the anger.

Natural disasters and other destructive events, such as war and disease, can greatly disrupt people's lives and even generate PTSD (post-traumatic stress disorder). As the name implies, people may become afflicted with high levels of anxiety after a traumatic event. Many of us, after a world-changing event (such as a natural disaster or a terrorist attack), might tend to catastrophize things. To manage your anxiety levels, **mindfulness** and the breathing techniques we discussed are great tools to help you regain some balance in life.

Our final topic for this section is examining yourself via the **ABC** and the scientific method to understand who you are, who you want to be, and your place in this world. By that, I mean to conduct self-exploration to shape yourself into someone you respect. Your beliefs, whether the ones inherited from your parents and your environment or the ones you created as time went by, shape your behaviors, your feelings, and your thoughts. You already know that. So, if you want to behave differently, think differently, and feel differently, you need to become aware of those beliefs and then change them. You have the necessary tools to get started.

Key Takeaways

- In this chapter, we discussed resilience in three main

areas of life: work, marriage and relationships, and life.

- To be accurate and flexible when thinking about the reasons why you were fired, use the **ABC model** and the scientific method to work on each hot, irrational belief.
- There is no way to tell if an employee is being prejudiced against you unless they clearly utter something. Avoid engaging in mind reading. Use any techniques you know to regain balance.
- Are your hot, irrational beliefs leading to issues with work-life balance? Use the **ABCDE model** to help you with your mental resilience and regain some peace of mind.
- If you find signs of a toxic work culture, first be honest and ask yourself if you're part of the problem. Second, find out if your beliefs are working for or against your goals. Third, decide if you're staying or leaving.
- Working on projects with few resources is a great way to increase your stress levels. To manage the stress, use the techniques we discussed in Chapter 3. Try to implement the other pieces of advice I provided at the end of the section.
- Lack of communication and fighting, among other factors, can end relationships. To improve communication, look for issues in the following filters: attention level, beliefs, feelings, and communication styles.
- Fighting can be divided into two main styles: **"what's wrong with you?"** and **"whose side are you on?"** The former is designed to hurt your partner's feelings; the latter is designed to understand and resolve issues.
- We established that some events basically generate an almost universal reaction, such as the death of loved ones, natural disasters, and war. The **ABC method** and

relaxation techniques will still help you with anxiety.

Chapter 4 is done. Now, let's move on to the last chapter of the book and its six-step guide to better resilience.

---

1. Curious about other countries? Access the source of the data at OECD's https://www.oecd.org/en/data/indicators/hours-worked.html .
2. Kat Boogaard, "5 Signs of a Toxic Work Culture (and What to Do if You're Stuck in One)," *Atlassian Work Life*, February 22, 2023, https://www.atlassian.com/blog/teamwork/toxic-work-culture .
3. Kurter, Heidi L. "Is Your Workplace Dysfunctional? Here Are The 5 Types Of Toxic Cultures." Forbes. Nov 30, 2021. https://www.forbes.com/sites/heidilynnekurter/2021/11/30/is-your-workplace-dysfunctional-here-are-the-5-types-of-toxic-cultures/?sh=252b65d52af4.
4. *Harvard Business Review*, https://hbr.org/ .
5. *Forbes Health*.. https://www.forbes.com/health/.
6. *American Psychological Association*. https://www.apa.org/ .
7. Markman, Howard J., Scott M. Stanley, and Susan L. Blumberg. *Fighting for Your Marriage: A Deluxe Revised Edition of the Classic Best-seller for Enhancing Marriage and Preventing Divorce.* (San Francisco: Jossey-Bass, 2010).
8. Gottman, John M., and Nan Silver. *The Seven Principles for Making Marriage Work: A Practical Guide from the Country's Foremost Relationship Expert.* (New York: Harmony Books, 1999).

Chapter Five

A Six-step Guide to Resilience

> Resilience is based on compassion for ourselves as well as compassion for others.
> —Sharon Salzberg, author and meditation teacher

You have read the whole book; now it's time for a short guide on improving your resilience. This guide is designed to help you start your journey if you haven't already. It won't cover every single possible way to improve your resilience. For that, you'll need to read up or do some research on your own. What follows is my own way of doing it.

Step 1: Create your Goals

Imagine you're free from any constraints. What would you like to accomplish? What would you like to do that you can't do now? What would change in your life if you had the mental resilience that you seek? Why? Examples of why could be "I'd like to feel less depressed when my mother falls ill," "I want to be able to resist dessert after dinner," or maybe "I'd like to control my anger whenever my boss criticizes me."

Once you have an idea of the reasons why you'd like to have more resilience, it will become easier for you to persevere when the situation becomes difficult. Writing your goals down in a notebook or note-taking app will allow you to think of mental resilience as something with real value and that can be applied to situations you experience.

Just having goals is not enough. You need to make sure you are set up for success. And how do you do this? By breaking down your goals into smaller ones. There are hundreds of books on setting goals. Find the one that resonates with you the most.

As an example of goal segmentation, let's say you'd like to stop smoking but don't think you have the grit to make it happen. Your irrational beliefs will probably play a role ("I can't just stop, it's impossible, and I'll probably just slip right back into it"), so be ready. To segment it and nurture mental resilience, start small. Instead of a pack a day, why not lower the total count to a manageable one, let's say nineteen or eighteen cigarettes a day for two weeks? In those two weeks, you'll do your best not to smoke more than the allotted quantity for the whole period. After that, lower the amount again by one or two units for two weeks again. Repeat the process until you no longer feel the need to smoke. That's just an example. Some people might get more value by stopping smoking cold turkey.

This segmentation approach is not flawless, mind you. Think about it. How would you segment the goal "become able to control my jealousy every time my wife spends time with her childhood friend?" You could try to spend a couple of hours with all three of you at a cafe to see the interaction and lower your jealousy. However, I believe working on the ABCDE for this example would yield better results.

Step 2: What if It Was a Gift?

You are probably very aware by now that our interpretations of adversities are the source of emotional pain, not the adversities themselves. How we react to adversities is what matters the most. One way to see obstacles in life is to reframe them as opportunities to learn something new rather than to allow yourself to become a powerless victim of your circumstances. The psychologist Robert Glover, I believe, urged people to see obstacles as opportunities to improve via the statement, "What if it was a gift?" In my personal experience, I'm less inclined to give up on my goals when faced with difficulties that challenge me and my mental resilience when I stop and ask myself that very question.

As an example, imagine that your goal is to find a romantic partner with the hopes of getting married and starting a family. You then download some dating apps or might try your luck at special events such as speed dating. Perhaps you prefer a more organic way of meeting new potential partners, so you ask friends to introduce coworkers, friends, or family members to you. After a few dates, none of the people you met want to see you again, at least romantically. You lose heart because it takes money, time, and mental energy to meet them via friends, contact them for the first time, message them back and forth, set dates, and finally meet them.

At this point, you have two options:

(a) get angry at them for wasting your time or feel sad because they don't want to meet you again,

or

(b) ask yourself, "What if it was a gift?" and keep trying.

Given the theme of this book, you probably decided that option (b) was the better one. I salute you if you did.

The second option allows you to see that the people who don't want to have a date with you again might not have been a good match in the long run. Had you tried to force your way into a relationship, you would have not only spent a lot of effort and time trying to convince that person to have a relationship with you, but it could also have resulted in misery for both of you. You'll probably never learn why they decided not to see you again, but by asking yourself if it was a gift, you reframe the whole situation: it was a good thing you didn't meet again. You'll have the chance to break down the last date with that person and try to see what you could have done better (maybe act less stiff, be more engaging in conversation, be more open-minded, be less needy, be more confident). You could ask friends for help with the analysis. But the important aspect I want you to keep in mind is to try and learn something new so you can make improvements.

So, whenever something "bad" happens to you, ask yourself, "What if it was a gift?" and take the opportunity to learn something new and improve. As you'll probably realize, this can be used for anything, especially for the things that are under your control. You just need to analyze the whole thing objectively.

Step 3: Try to Control Your Negative Emotions

The next step involves trying to control negative emotions that appear when faced with adversity. The keyword here is "try" because, as you know, you can't stop your brain from making them. By trying to control these negative emotions, you stop them from overtaking your thought processes, which can lead to inaction or, worse yet, making decisions you may regret. Your best bet is to analyze your negative emotions through the **ABC** (or **ABCDE**) lens. If you need to use the other techniques mentioned in this book—the scientific method, for example—go ahead, as they will help you with mental resilience.

Let's suppose you saw a strange message from someone you don't know on your significant other's phone. Your mind might come up with all kinds of crazy thoughts and, with them, negative emotions, such as jealousy, anger, and sadness. If you use the **ABC** or the scientific method here, you'll probably come up with reasonable ideas as to what the message means and make rational decisions. That might mean talking with your spouse about the message rather than making hasty decisions, like hiring a private eye or starting a fight. Be aware that the objective here is not to delude yourself with wishful thinking. It could well mean the origin of a rift between you two, one that could lead to a separation.

Alternatively, the message could have been a mistake caused by a wrong phone number or recipient. Or maybe your spouse was the target of a practical joke or smear campaign. And you learned the truth by behaving rationally and talking to him rather than letting your emotions, irrational beliefs, and negative thoughts take over.

Step 4: Use Guided Imagery and Visualization

You already know what guided imagery is: simulating or creating sensory perceptions through mental images to achieve a heightened sense of relaxation. Guess what? You can use it to improve your emotional resilience as well.

Athletes and business people use a simplified form of guided imagery to rehearse before an important moment in their lives. Instead of imagining unimportant details of a situation (temperature, sounds, and tastes, for example, are rarely important for the success of a presentation or a championship), they visualize being successful, priming their brains for improved performance. They also visualize effectively dealing with possible issues that may arise, enabling them to react faster.

Visualize yourself being successful before major life events. Imagine yourself beating the odds. Create a guided visualization with the feelings, thoughts, and behaviors that would arise if you were to deal with tough situations and the different ways things could go south. In other words, imagine contingency plans.

We don't always know when obstacles in life will challenge us. But if you expect something negative to happen, like being denied a loan at a bank, a raise from your boss, or a second or third date with a potential partner, visualize yourself successfully dealing with probable issues along the process and the negative emotions that may arise if failure is unavoidable.

Step 5: Dispute Irrational Beliefs and Unhelpful Thoughts

You're probably well aware that increasing mental resilience is not that simple. It's important to know how to deal with irrational beliefs, **iceberg beliefs**, and cognitive distortions. Use the tools we have discussed in this book, such as the **ABC** and the scientific method, every time you see that your brain is being unhelpful in achieving your goals related to mental resilience.

However, to use those tools when you need them most, i.e., during a crisis, you need practice. You surely don't expect to be able to perform complex movements of a sport or other physical activities proficiently without having practiced them before. The same applies to the act of disputing your beliefs, both irrational and hidden, and your unhelpful thinking patterns. Review Chapters 2 and 3 if you need a refresher.

Don't worry if you can't successfully deal with every adversity or irrational belief. Expect some failed experiments in the beginning. Acknowledge not only your weaknesses but also your strengths, like your innate ability to adapt and improve. Pay no heed to the inner voice nagging whenever you make a mistake or fail to perform to your expectations. Negative self-talk is a form of cognitive distortion, sometimes originating from overgeneralization or personalization. It usually involves catastrophic thinking, black-and-white thinking, jumping to conclusions, or all of them. Typical examples go along the lines of "Everything I do goes wrong," "Everybody thinks I'm an idiot," "No one cares about what I think," "I'll never succeed," or any other variation. Learn to silence that inner critic, or at least learn to recognize it so you can dispute its arguments.

Step 6: Create a Habit and Celebrate your Victories

Having healthy habits allows you to better control your impulses and power through discomfort and adversities, as well as delay gratification. Instead of impulsively reacting to obstacles and regretting that decision later, why not create a healthy habit that allows you to understand your emotions, thoughts, and behaviors BEFORE taking action? That could be taking notes and analyzing the event through the **ABCDE** lens, going out for a jog, or hitting the library for a study session.

All right, so how do I go about creating healthy habits? In my previous book, *The Mindful Path*, I described an effective method to help readers create the habit of meditation. If you haven't read it yet, here's a very simplified version:

1. Set a clearly defined goal

2. Keep the habit short and simple

3. Celebrate

The first necessary item involves creating a SMART goal related to the new habit you want to adopt. SMART goals are: **Specific, Measurable, Achievable, Relevant, and Time-bound**. Research online on your favorite search engine how to create SMART goals. If you don't know what it is already, you won't regret it. I promise.

The second item of habit creation involves segmenting your habit into simple, short, and easily digestible chunks, which I already mentioned in Step 1. Segmenting goals and habits are overlapping skills. If you want to start running and eventually attempt a marathon, you might want to avoid going all out and run twenty-six miles (about forty-two kilometers) in the first session. That would be suicide. You would start small, with achievable stages, and have a deadline in mind. If you're struggling to even get out and run, why not segment the first part of the habit? For example, run for ten minutes in the first week, then fifteen minutes in the second, and so on and so forth, all the way to an hour-long session. Then, you create new goals and make sure you can achieve them.

The third item is to celebrate every time you perform a segmented part of the habit. In the previous example, let's say you ran for ten minutes in the first session. Great, now celebrate this initial achievement. Eat a tasty fruit, listen to your favorite song, take a relaxing bath, or call a family member. You can high-five yourself, do a fist pump, or say "Awesome!" to yourself. Anything that creates warm, fuzzy feelings inside is valid. You should do your best to celebrate at three distinct moments: as soon as you remember to act, during the action, and right after you finish performing it. The last one, immediately after, is a must in case you're a forgetful person.

If you need more details, I suggest looking at your local library, bookstore, or favorite ebook marketplace for resources on how to create habits that stick and help you with your goals.

CONCLUSION

A workplace resilience study from 2020[1] conducted in the United States provides some interesting insights:

- 19% of the workers studied were considered highly resilient, against 81% who were less resilient (vulnerable).
- Workers who love what they do, independent of their proficiency levels, are 3.9 times more likely to be highly resilient.
- What you do at work has an impact on your levels of resilience, with knowledge workers more likely to be highly resilient than workers who perform repetitive tasks.
- Although men tend to be more resilient than women, the data shows that the statistical difference can be ignored and is not meaningful.
- Age is not a factor in workplace-related resilience, with 14% of Gen Z and 13% of Boomers being highly resilient.

The full report of that study states that the people who experienced COVID-19 firsthand had better resilience than those who didn't. The explanation is that "fear of the unknown is one of the most powerful negative influences on people's mental well-being" (page 15). Once they experienced it, it was no longer an unknown disease, and that proved to them how resilient they were. The authors believe that "facing challenges realistically and openly will build people's capacity for resilience."

What does this tell you, dear reader? To me, it shows the reality that I mentioned in the first chapter: resilience is a by-product of how you deal with adversities, that is, the thoughts, the feelings, and the behaviors you display. This study, although focused on workers, allows us to extrapolate some of its findings to life. The first thing is that to increase your resilience, you have to experience adversities personally. The second is that the more realistic your beliefs related to those adversities are, together with being proactive in facing those adversities, the higher your resilience will be.

It all makes sense. Can you say with a high level of confidence that life is easy and devoid of difficulties? Do you know anyone who hasn't faced difficult challenges in life? Among the most mentally tough people you know, how many of them have unrealistic expectations of the outcomes of the difficulties they face? How many of them hold irrational beliefs and still have high resilience?

The thesis of this book is that, indeed, you can increase your mental resilience. You do need to work hard to achieve it. You may have to go through very difficult situations to get there. Fortunately, there are tools and techniques available for that purpose. Remember, how you interpret adversity is the source of misery, not the adversity itself. If you believe an obstacle is just a temporary setback and it's an opportunity to learn something new or improve your condition, then you're well on your way to being mentally and emotionally resilient.

Let's quickly go over the contents of this book. In Chapter 1, we talked about the definition of resilience, the benefits of being resilient, the source of irrationality, the most common sources of disturbance, and the meaning of REBT.

In Chapter 2, we strove to understand one of the most important tools in our skillset: the **ABC model**. We also talked about thinking traps (aka cognitive distortions or unhelpful thinking patterns), **iceberg beliefs**, and ways to uncover them.

In Chapter 3, we discussed the scientific method and how to use it to dispute your irrational beliefs, as proposed by Albert Ellis. After that, we went over the **ABCDE method**, a variation of the **ABC model**, which Ellis also proposed. We then discussed a list of common irrational beliefs. I also presented a list of techniques you can use to calm yourself down when your emotions get out of control, for example, the **4-7-8 breathing technique** and **mindfulness**.

In Chapter 4, we talked about challenges people face in three spheres: the workplace, relationships, and life in general. The objective was to discuss ways you can become more resilient when facing common situations in those spheres.

In Chapter 5, we went over six steps to augment your mental resilience.

Over to You

Congrats! You arrived at the end of the book. You learned a lot about resilience. Pat yourself on the back. But don't get too comfortable. Now is the time to actually take the knowledge you acquired from this book for a spin.

Get a notebook and a pencil or an app such as Microsoft OneNote, Google Keep, or Apple Notes. Reread Chapter 5. Review tough situations from your past and think about irrational beliefs and how they affected your thoughts and behaviors. How would you dispute them?

What I want you to do is to practice, practice, and practice some more. That way, you'll be ready to face your next challenge. Good luck!

I hope you enjoyed reading *The Art of Mental Resilience* as much as I enjoyed writing it. If so, please hop online and post a review! Reviews turn sad authors into happy authors. Oh, and I personally read all reviews. It doesn't have to be a lengthy one either; one or two lines is more than enough and greatly appreciated!

Also, if you'd like to hear about new books and promotions, access my website at https://ivesymurai.com and consider subscribing to my newsletter. Thank you!

---

1. Hayes, Mary, Frances Chumney, and Marcus Buckingham. 2020. "Workplace Resilience Study: full research report". ADP Research. https://www.adpri.org/assets/workplace-resilience-study/.

GLOSSARY

4-7-8 Breathing Technique: A relaxation exercise involving inhaling for 4 seconds, holding the breath for 7 seconds, and exhaling for 8 seconds, aimed at reducing anxiety.

4-4-4-4 Breathing Technique: A breathing method that consists of inhaling for 4 seconds, holding for 4 seconds, exhaling for 4 seconds, and pausing for 4 seconds, which helps to calm the mind and regulate breath.

ABCDE: An extension of the original ABC model in cognitive therapy, incorporating Disputation of beliefs and Effect to enhance understanding of how beliefs influence emotional responses.

Arbitrary Inference: A cognitive distortion that occurs when conclusions are drawn without sufficient evidence or justification, often resulting in negative interpretations of situations.

Cognitive Behavioral Therapy (CBT): A type of psychotherapy focused on identifying and altering negative thought patterns and behaviors to improve emotional regulation and develop effective coping strategies.

Conditional Self-Esteem (CSE): A form of self-esteem contingent upon external factors or specific conditions, leading individuals to feel positive about themselves only when they meet particular standards or expectations.

Cool Thoughts: Rational and constructive thoughts that foster healthy emotions and behaviors, characterized by a calm and logical perspective, devoid of ratings or judgments.

Dichotomous Thinking: A cognitive distortion characterized by viewing situations in black-and-white terms, without recognizing any middle ground, which can lead to extreme evaluations and reactions.

Gridlock: A term introduced by Dr. John Gottman referring to a state in a relationship where partners cannot resolve perpetual problems, often resulting in repeated arguments and frustration.

Guided Imagery: A relaxation technique that employs mental images and visualization to create a sense of calm and enhance emotional well-being.

Iceberg Beliefs: Deeply ingrained convictions or assumptions that influence an individual's thoughts and behaviors, often affecting emotional responses without conscious awareness.

Irrational Beliefs: Erroneous or unfounded beliefs that can lead to unhealthy emotions and behaviors, frequently involving unrealistic expectations or catastrophic thinking.

Magnification: Also referred to as catastrophizing, this cognitive distortion involves exaggerating negative aspects of oneself, others, or events, resulting in heightened anxiety and distress.

Meditation: A practice involving focused thought, often utilizing techniques like mindfulness or guided imagery, to achieve mental clarity, emotional calm, and self-awareness.

Mindfulness: A mental practice focusing on the present moment with acceptance and without judgment, promoting awareness of thoughts, feelings, and sensations.

Minimization: The act of downplaying positive aspects of oneself, another person, or a specific event, which often skews perception and diminishes self-worth.

Musturbation: A term coined by Albert Ellis to describe the tendency to impose unrealistic demands on oneself or others, often resulting in feelings of frustration and inadequacy.

Negative Mental Filtering: A cognitive distortion in which individuals concentrate solely on the negative aspects of a situation, ignoring the positive, leading to a pessimistic outlook.

Perpetual Problems: Ongoing issues in relationships that are challenging to resolve due to differing core values or needs, often necessitating partners to learn how to manage and navigate them.

Positive Mental Filtering: A cognitive approach where individuals emphasize and focus on the positive aspects of a situation, often to the detriment of all negative ones. Commonly used to explain addictions.

Pranayama: A yogic practice involving various breath control techniques designed to promote physical and mental well-being.

Progressive Muscle Relaxation (PMR): A relaxation technique involving the tensing and then relaxing of different muscle groups in the body to alleviate physical tension and stress.

Rational Beliefs: Logical and realistic beliefs that contribute to healthy emotional responses and positive behaviors, generally grounded in reality and promoting resilience.

Rational Emotive Behavior Therapy (REBT): A form of cognitive-behavioral therapy developed by Albert Ellis, focusing on transforming irrational beliefs into rational ones to enhance emotional well-being.

Selective Abstraction: A cognitive distortion in which an individual fixates on one detail of a situation while disregarding the larger context, often leading to negative conclusions.

SMART Goals: A framework for setting effective goals that are Specific, Measurable, Achievable, Relevant, and Time-bound, aiding individuals in clarifying their objectives and tracking progress.

Solvable Problems: Issues within relationships that can be resolved through discussion and compromise, enabling partners to reach mutually agreeable solutions.

Three-Part Breath: A breathing technique that entails deeply inhaling into the abdomen, expanding the ribcage, and filling the upper lungs, which fosters relaxation and mindfulness.

Unconditional Life-Acceptance (ULA): The acceptance of life and its inherent challenges without conditions, fostering a more positive and resilient mindset.

Unconditional Other-Acceptance (UOA): The acceptance of others regardless of their behaviors, opinions, or actions, promoting healthier relationships and minimizing interpersonal conflict.

Unconditional Self-Acceptance (USA): The practice of fully accepting oneself without conditions, enabling individuals to embrace both their flaws and strengths.

Warm Thoughts: Positive, supportive, and affirming thoughts that enhance emotional well-being and encourage healthy coping mechanisms. Warm thoughts include wishes and desires, likes and dislikes.

"What's Wrong With You?": A combative, scathing approach to conflict characterized by criticism of minor mistakes, aimed at hurting a partner's feelings.

"Whose Side Are You On?": A constructive approach to conflict that seeks understanding and resolution while keeping complaints specific and free from ambiguity, encouraging inquiry and collaboration.

References

American Psychological Association. "Coping with Stress at Work." 2018. https://www.apa.org/topics/healthy-workplaces/work-stress.

Basso, Julia C, Alexandra McHale, Victoria Ende, Douglas J Oberlin, and Wendy A Suzuki. 2019. "Brief, Daily Meditation Enhances Attention, Memory, Mood, and Emotional Regulation in Non-experienced Meditators." *Behav Brain Res*. Jan 1;356:208-220. doi: 10.1016/j.bbr.2018.08.023. Epub 2018 Aug 25. PMID: 30153464.

Beck, Aaron T. 1963. "Thinking and Depression: I. Idiosyncratic Content and Cognitive Distortions." *Archives of General Psychiatry*, 9(4), 324–333.

———. 1976. *Cognitive Therapy and the Emotional Disorders*. (New York: International Universities Press, 1976).

Beck, Judith S. 2012. "Annual Reviews Conversations Presents: A Conversation with Aaron T. Beck." *Annual Reviews*. Retrieved from: https://www.annualreviews.org/userimages/ContentEditor/1351004835908/AaronTBeckTranscript.pdf.

Blackburn Ivy M, Kate M Eunson. 1989. "A content analysis of thoughts and emotions elicited from depressed patients during cognitive therapy." *Br J Med Psychol*. 1989 Mar;62 (Pt 1):23-33. doi: 10.1111/j.2044-8341.1989.tb02807.x. PMID: 2706195.

Blake, Emily, Keith S Dobson, Amanda R Sheptycki, and Martin Drapeau. 2016. "The Relationship Between Depression Severity and Cognitive Errors." *American Journal of Psychotherapy*, 70, 203-221. DOI: 10.1176/appi.psychotherapy.2016.70.2.203.

Boogard, Kat. 2022. "5 Signs of a Toxic Work Culture (and What to Do if You're Stuck in One)." *Atlassian*. https://www.atlassian.com/blog/teamwork/toxic-work-culture.

Burns, David D. 2020. *Feeling Great: The Revolutionary New Treatment for Depression and Anxiety*. PESI Publishing.

Cleveland Clinic. "Guided Imagery: How It Helps With Stress & Managing Anxiety." Cleveland Clinic Health Essentials, September 13, 2022. https://health.clevelandclinic.org/guided-imagery-how-it-helps-with-stress-managing-anxiety/.

David, Daniel, Carmen Cotet, Silviu Matu, Cristina Mogoase, Simona Stefan. 2018. "50 Years of Rational-Emotive and Cognitive-Behavioral Therapy: A Systematic Review and Meta-Analysis." *J Clin Psychol.* 2018 Mar;74(3):304-318. doi: 10.1002/jclp.22514. Epub 2017 Sep 12. PMID: 28898411; PMCID: PMC5836900.

Davidson, Richard J, Jon Kabat-Zinn, Jessica Schumacher, Melissa Rosenkranz, Daniel Muller, Saki F Santorelli, Ferris Urbanowski, Anne Harrington, Katherine Bonus, and John F Sheridan. 2003. "Alterations in Brain and Immune Function Produced by Mindfulness Meditation." *Psychosom Med.* Jul-Aug;65(4):564-70. doi: 10.1097/01.psy.0000077505.67574.e3. PMID: 12883106.

Davis, Melissa, and Nicole Wosinski. 2011. "Cognitive Errors as Predictors of Adaptive and Maladaptive Perfectionism in Children." *Journal of Rational-emotive & Cognitive-behavior Therapy*. 30. 1-13. 10.1007/s10942-011-0129-1.

Dusek, Jeffry A, Patricia L Hibberd, Beverly Buczynski, Bei-Hung Chang, Kathryn C Dusek, Jennifer M Johnston, Ann L Wohlhueter, Herbert Benson, and Randall M Zusman. 2008. "Stress Management Versus Lifestyle Modification on Systolic Hypertension and Medication Elimination: a Randomized Trial." *J Altern Complement Med.* Mar;14(2):129-38. doi: 10.1089/acm.2007.0623. PMID: 18315510.

Eckhardt, Christopher I, and Howard Kassinove. 1998. "Articulated Cognitive Distortions and Cognitive Deficiencies in Maritally Violent Men." *Journal of Cognitive Psychotherapy*, 12(3), 231–250.

Ellis, Albert. 1956. "Rational Psychotherapy and Individual Psychology," presented at the American Psychological Association Conference.

———. 1962. *Reason and Emotion in Psychotherapy*. New York: Lyle Stuart.

———. 2006. *How to Stubbornly Refuse to Make Yourself Miserable About Anything-yes, Anything!* Kensington Publishing Corp. New York, NY.

Epstein, Robert. "The Prince of Reason," January 1, 2001. https://www.psychologytoday.com/intl/articles/200101/the-prince-reason.

Gottman, John M., and Nan Silver. *The Seven Principles for Making Marriage Work: A Practical Guide from the Country's Foremost Relationship Expert*. (New York: Harmony Books, 1999).

Goyal Rajni, Hem Lata, Lily Walia, and Manjit K Narula. 2014. "Effect of pranayama on rate pressure product in mild hypertensives." *Int J Appl Basic Med Res*. Jul;4(2):67-71. doi: 10.4103/2229-516X.136776. PMID: 25143878; PMCID: PMC4137644.

Harorani, Mehdi, Fahimeh Davodabady, Behnam Masmouei, and Niloofar Barati. 2020. "The effect of progressive muscle relaxation on anxiety and sleep quality in burn patients: A randomized clinical trial." *Burns*. Volume 46, Issue 5, Pages 1107-1113. https://doi.org/10.1016/j.burns.2019.11.021.

Hayes, Mary, Frances Chumney, and Marcus Buckingham. 2020. "Workplace Resilience Study: full research report". ADP Research. https://www.adpri.org/assets/workplace-resilience-study/.

Jacobson, Edmund. 1938. *Progressive Relaxation: A Physiological and Clinical Investigation of Muscular States and Their Significance in Psychology and Medical Practice.* (Chicago: University of Chicago Press).

Jager-Hyman, Shari, Amy Cunningham, Amy Wenzel, Stephanie Mattei, Gregory K Brown, and Aaron T Beck. 2014. "Cognitive Distortions and Suicide Attempts." *Cognit Ther*

Res. Aug 1;38(4):369-374. doi: 10.1007/s10608-014-9613-0. PMID: 25294949; PMCID: PMC4185206.

Kurter, Heidi L. 2021. "Is Your Workplace Dysfunctional? Here Are The 5 Types Of Toxic Cultures." Forbes. Nov 30.

Lin, Yanli, William D Eckerle, Ling W Peng, and Jason S Moser. 2019. "On Variation in Mindfulness Training: A Multimodal Study of Brief Open Monitoring Meditation on Error Monitoring" *Brain Sciences* 9, no. 9: 226. https://doi.org/10.3390/brainsci9090226.

Markman, Howard J, Scott M Stanley, and Susan L Blumberg. 2010. *Fighting for Your Marriage: A Deluxe Revised Edition of the Classic Best-seller for Enhancing Marriage and Preventing Divorce*. Jossey-Bass. 3rd ed.

Mateu, Margarita, Olga Alda, Maria-Del-Mar Inda, Cesar Margarit, Raquel Ajo, Domingo Morales, Carlos J van-der Hofstadt, and Ana M Peiró. 2018. "Randomized, Controlled, Crossover Study of Self-administered Jacobson Relaxation in Chronic, Nonspecific, Low-back Pain." *Altern Ther Health Med*. Nov; 24(6):22-30. PMID: 30982021.

Meister, Alyson, Bonnie H Cheng, Nele Dael, and Franciska Krings. 2022. "How to Recover from Work Stress, According to Science." Harvard Business Review. July 05. https://hbr.org/2022/07/how-to-recover-from-work-stress-according-to-science.

Merakou, Kyriakoula, Konstantinos Tsoukas, Giorgio Stavrinos, Eirini Amanaki, Antonia Daleziou, Ntina Kourmousi, Georgia Stamatelopoulou, Evi Spourdalaki, and Anastasia Barbouni. 2019. "The Effect of Progressive Muscle Relaxation on Emotional Competence: Depression-Anxiety-Stress, Sense of Coherence, Health-Related Quality of Life, and Well-Being of Unemployed People in Greece: An Intervention Study." *Explore* (NY). Jan-Feb;15(1):38-46. doi: 10.1016/j.explore.2018.08.001. Epub 2018 Aug 20. PMID: 30228090.

Meyer, Bianca, Armin Keller, Hans-Georg Wöhlbier, Claudia H Overath, Britta Müller, and Peter Kropp. 2016. "Progressive muscle relaxation reduces migraine frequency and normalizes amplitudes of contingent negative variation (CNV)." *J Headache Pain*. 2016;17:37. doi:

10.1186/s10194-016-0630-0. Epub 2016 Apr 18. PMID: 27090417; PMCID: PMC4835398.

Novaes, Morgana M, Fernanda Palhano-Fontes, Heloisa Onias, Katia C Andrade, Bruno Lobão-Soares, Tiago Arruda-Sanchez, Elisa H Kozasa, Danilo F Santaella, Draulio B de Araujo. 2020. "Effects of Yoga Respiratory Practice (Bhastrika pranayama) on Anxiety, Affect, and Brain Functional Connectivity and Activity: A Randomized Controlled Trial." *Front Psychiatry*. May 21;11:467. doi: 10.3389/fpsyt.2020.00467. PMID: 32528330; PMCID: PMC7253694.

Pittman, Catherine M, and Elizabeth M Karle. 2015. *Rewire Your Anxious Brain: How to Use the Neuroscience of Fear to End Anxiety, Panic, and Worry*. New Harbinger Publications. — 1st ed.

Reivich, Karen, and Andrew Shatté. 2003. *The resilience factor: 7 Keys to Finding Your Inner Strength and Overcoming Life's Hurdles*. Harmony —1st ed.

Schulz, Enrico, Anne Stankewitz, Anderson M Winkler, Stephanie Irving, Viktor Witkovský, and Irene Tracey. 2020. "Ultra-high-field imaging reveals increased whole brain connectivity underpins cognitive strategies that attenuate pain." *eLife* Sep 2;9:e55028. doi: 10.7554/eLife.55028. PMID: 32876049; PMCID: PMC7498261.

Shahab, Lion, Bidyut K Sarkar, and Robert West. 2013. "The Acute Effects of Yogic Breathing Exercises on Craving and Withdrawal Symptoms in Abstaining Smokers." Psychopharmacology (Berl). 2013 Feb;225(4):875-82. doi: 10.1007/s00213-012-2876-9. Epub 2012 Sep 20. PMID: 22993051.

Shankarappa V, Prashanth P, Annamalai P, and Malhotra V. 2012. "The Short Term Effect of Pranayama on the Lung Parameters." *Journal of Clinical and Diagnostic Research*. February, 15. Vol-6(1): 27-30. https://www.jcdr.net/articles/PDF/1861/6%20-%203476.(A).pdf.

Shastri, Vasant V, Alex Hankey, Bhawna Sharma, and Sanjib Patra. 2017. "Investigation of Yoga Pranayama and Vedic Mathematics on Mindfulness, Aggression and Emotion Regulation." *International Journal of Yoga*. Sep-Dec;10(3):138-144. doi: 10.4103/0973-6131.213470. PMID: 29422744; PMCID: PMC5793008.

Sheu, Sheila, Barbara L Irvin, Huey-Shyan Lin, and Chun-Lin Mar. 2003. "Effects of progressive muscle relaxation on blood pressure and psychosocial status for clients with essential hypertension in Taiwan." *Holist Nurs Pract*. Jan-Feb;17(1):41-7. doi: 10.1097/00004650-200301000-00009. PMID: 12597674.

Silva, Lauren. 2023. "How To Deal With Stress At Work, According To Experts." Forbes. Sep 28. https://www.forbes.com/health/mind/how-to-deal-with-stress-at-work/.

Whitbourne, Susan K. 2012. "The definitive guide to guilt." Psychology Today. Aug 11.

Whitfield, Tim, Thorsten Barnhofer, Rebecca Acabchuk, Avi Cohen, Michael Lee, Marco Scholsser, Eider M Arenaza-Urquijo, et al. 2022. "The Effect of Mindfulness-based Programs on Cognitive Function in Adults: A Systematic Review and Meta-analysis." *Neuropsychol Rev*. Sep;32(3):677-702. doi: 10.1007/s11065-021-09519-y. Epub 2021 Aug 4. PMID: 34350544; PMCID: PMC9381612.

About the Author

Ives Y. Murai is a writer and an English teacher. His goal is to help people facing difficulties in life through his books. He wishes to write a hundred books on a wide range of topics before he turns sixty years old. He strives to write informative and easy-to-understand self-help books. When he's not reading personal development books, he can be found playing computer games or exercising at the local health club. He lives in Brazil with his family and two pets: Moggy the Siamese cat and Bob the dog.

He can be reached at ives.murai@gmail.com.

ALSO BY

TAMING ANXIETY: HANDLE WORRY, COPE WITH FEARS, MANAGE PANIC ATTACKS, AND GET A GRIP ON NEGATIVE THOUGHTS.

Learn to manage fear and anxiety on your own.

Buy it now on Amazon! Click here.

The Mindful Path: How to Nail the Habit of Meditation and Decrease Stress in Everyday Life

Learn how to meditate and use mindfulness to reduce stress and find peace.

Buy it now on Amazon! Click here.

Book Cover by Tiago Pereira.

Made in the USA
Columbia, SC
09 July 2025

60533027R00087